DRAGONS, TIGERS AND BAMBOO

OLIVER IMPEY
CHRISTIAAN J.A. JÖRG
CHARLES MASON

DRAGONS, TIGERS AND BAMBOO

JAPANESE PORCELAIN AND ITS IMPACT IN EUROPE

THE MACDONALD COLLECTION

DOUGLAS & McINTYRE
D&M PUBLISHERS INC.
Vancouver/Toronto/Berkeley

09 10 11 12 13 5 4 3 2 1

Douglas & McIntyre
A division of D&M Publishers Inc.
2323 Quebec Street, Suite 201, Vancouver, B.C., Canada V5T 4S7
www.dmpibooks.com

Gardiner Museum
111 Queen's Park, Toronto, Ontario, Canada M5S 2C7
www.gardinermuseum.com

Library and Archives Canada Cataloguing in Publication

George R. Gardiner Museum of Ceramic Art. Macdonald Collection.
Dragons, tigers and bamboo : Japanese porcelain and its impact in Europe.

Includes bibliographical references.
ISBN 978-1-55365-434-6

1. Porcelain, Japanese—Catalogs. 2. Porcelain, Japanese. 3. George R. Gardiner Museum of Ceramic Art. Macdonald Collection—Catalogs. I. Title.
NK4567.G46 2009 738.20952'074713541
C2008-907701-6

Editing by Meg Taylor
Jacket and text design by George Vaitkunas
Jacket photograph by Brian Boyle
Photos by Brian Boyle

Printed and bound in China by C & C Offset Printing Co. Ltd.
Printed on acid-free paper
Distributed in the U.S. by Publishers Group West

We gratefully acknowledge the financial support of the Canada Council for the Arts, the British Columbia Arts Council, the Province of British Columbia through the Book Publishing Tax Credit and the Government of Canada through the Book Publishing Industry Development Program (BPIDP) for our publishing activities.

page 2, Fig. 1: Dish with Solitary Boatman. Japan, Arita, c. 1670. D: 21 cm

CONTENTS

DIRECTOR'S PREFACE

THIS BOOK WAS MADE POSSIBLE by the generosity and hard work of many people. Foremost, of course, are Bill and Molly Anne Macdonald. Over the past twenty-three years, Bill and Molly Anne have formed an extraordinary collection of ceramic objects that illustrate the development of porcelain in Japan during the seventeenth and eighteenth centuries and the impact Japanese porcelain had on the development of ceramics in Europe and England during the eighteenth and nineteenth centuries. The Macdonald Collection is unquestionably the best of its kind in Canada and one of the best of its kind in the world. The gift of this collection to the Gardiner Museum is among the most generous donations of cultural property that the museum has ever received. It represents a legacy that will continue to enrich and inform museum visitors for generations to come.

Crucial funding for the book was provided by the E. Rhodes and Leona B. Carpenter Foundation, Canadian Pacific Railway, Richard and Elizabeth Currie, the Honourable H.N.R. Jackman, the Japan Foundation, the Jarislowsky Foundation, Manulife Financial, Osler, Hoskin & Harcourt LLP, George and Letha Whyte and an anonymous donor. Their generous support has made it possible to publish the Macdonald Collection and thereby share it with the world beyond the Gardiner Museum.

Thanks are due to the entire Douglas & McIntyre team, including Scott McIntyre, Scott Steedman, George Vaitkunas, Meg Taylor and Ruth Gaskill for producing the book. Brian Boyle photographed the Macdonald Collection for the book.

The Museum is honoured to feature contributions from the late Dr. Oliver Impey and Prof. Dr. Christiaan J.A. Jörg, two of the leading experts on Japanese export art and its impact in the West. Their participation is a tribute to the Macdonald Collection.

At the Gardiner Museum, Chief Curator Charles Mason worked closely with the Macdonalds to select the objects that are illustrated in this book. His extensive expertise and intellectual curiosity are reflected in his essay, which provides an introduction to Japanese porcelain. His interpretive text and captions provide a meaningful context for the highlights of the Macdonald Collection included here. He also coordinated the entire project, helping to edit the essays from Oliver Impey and Christiaan Jörg and working with the designer and editor on all aspects of the book. Major Gifts Officer Peter Wambera and Collections Manager Christina Green should also be acknowledged for their contributions to this publication.

ALEXANDRA MONTGOMERY
EXECUTIVE DIRECTOR
GARDINER MUSEUM OF CERAMIC ART

THE MACDONALD COLLECTION

THERE MUST BE ALMOST AS MANY REASONS for collecting objects as there are types of objects to collect. Some collectors, often the most interesting, have some fixed purpose or purposes, which may become clear to the collector only during the formation of the collection. Few collectors will not be sidetracked occasionally by some object that falls outside the range of their collection but is just too marvellous to miss. Equally, for some collectors only the latest acquisition is a triumph, whereas for others the greatest satisfaction is to be had in the building up of a well-defined collection. No collection could ever be complete (appalling thought!), but could expand indefinitely. Most collectors solve this problem by trading up, but others are simply careful buyers.

Bill and Molly Anne Macdonald began this collection, I believe, for the best of all possible reasons—namely, the simple love of the objects themselves. To have started with Kakiemon is, to my deeply prejudiced eye, more than praiseworthy. Their friendship with the great London-based ceramics dealer Bob Williams enabled them to expand their horizons in the direction that is the strength of the collection today: that is, toward the European porcelain that was influenced by Kakiemon. Later, the Macdonalds grew to love the seemingly simple Shoki-Imari and from this began an interest in the origins and development of Japanese porcelain.

These two themes predominate in this collection, and the whole forms a marvellous comparative study of what Japanese porcelain is and how it came to be so influential in Europe. Wisely, the Macdonalds have avoided going too far afield: I entirely understand their reluctance to venture into the vast minefield of the Imari. Thus the collection covers a large but not impossibly broad field. In recent years, however, I have noticed a tentative venture into Nabeshima and the related Matsugatani, some of the most beautiful and inventive porcelains in the world.

OLIVER IMPEY

JUNE 2005

FROM THE COLLECTORS, MOLLY ANNE AND BILL MACDONALD

IN APRIL 1984, the newly built George R. Gardiner Museum of Ceramic Art opened its doors to the public. Because I planned to retire that spring, I had already joined the volunteer committee. The following September I began training as a museum docent. A new world of interest, pleasure and friendship opened for Bill and me.

For years we had possessed a casual interest in nineteenth-century "china" and contemporary studio pottery. With docent training, we discovered ceramic history from the third century BCE to the late twentieth century and felt as though a whole new world had opened to us. What particularly caught my interest was an example of the transmigration of design, a process that had fascinated me for several years. I saw this process in European copies of seventeenth-century Japanese export porcelain in the Kakiemon style. The Japanese work, in turn, references not only Chinese models but also designs from Mughal India and even ancient Greece.

Bill's work had more than once taken us to Japan, where I was charmed by the Japanese love of nature. Their preference for simplicity, at times extending almost to naïveté, appealed to me, as did their use of asymmetry and negative space. These characteristics are to be found in Kakiemon ware, and the sparsely painted freehand decoration admirably reflects the good humour that seems to be a part of Japanese life.

As the secret of making porcelain spread through central Europe and Britain in the eighteenth century, Kakiemon-style imports supplied inspiration for shapes and decoration to workers in the new factories. I like to think that in each country, decorators imbued their copies of the familiar patterns with something of their national personality. The French brought grace and femininity; the Dutch work has a sturdy, straightforward style. German decorators were rigorously exact in their copying, whereas the English often mixed Kakiemon and Chinese influences to create highly individual pieces.

Our collection now has two prongs: the original comparison of Japanese Kakiemon shapes and decoration with the wares they inspired in Europe, and a lightly sketched survey of the astonishing variety and artistry of seventeenth-century Arita production.

Putting this collection together over the past twenty-three years has given Bill and me a vast amount of stimulation and pleasure. We owe affectionate thanks to many people who helped us with their advice and friendship. Helen and

Fig. 2
PAIR OF DISHES WITH SCATTERED BLOSSOM DESIGN
Japan, Arita, c. 1700
D: 18.3 cm G04.18.42.1-2
TEAPOT WITH SCATTERED BLOSSOM DESIGN
Germany, Meissen factory, c. 1728–31
L: 18.2 cm

George Gardiner inspired us with their extensive collection. Meredith Chilton, Bob Williams and Oliver Impey set our feet on the right paths to effective collecting. Others who helped us find interesting pieces were Errol Manners, Richard Barker, Yoshi Imaizumi, Tokuji Imai and Nicole Rousmaniere, all of whom are passionately committed to extending the bounds of ceramic knowledge.

Finally, we owe a great debt of gratitude to Oliver Impey's friend and colleague Christiaan Jörg for the essay he has contributed to this book, and to Charles Mason, Chief Curator at the Gardiner Museum, who presents a stimulating overview of the historical, social and cultural background to the development of Japanese porcelain.

MOLLY ANNE MACDONALD

WE DID NOT SET OUT to build a collection on the scale we did. Nor did we have any thought of leaving what we collected to a museum. We simply acquired a growing number of individual pieces that we liked for themselves and because they reflected a Japanese and Western inter-influence theme, which pleased us. In the early 1990s, when the collection was probably less than a third of what it is now, Oliver Impey told us that we had created something extraordinary. He said the only comparable collections were at the Idemitsu Museum in Tokyo, the Rijksmuseum in Amsterdam and the Syz Collection in Washington, D.C. We gradually concluded that the way to preserve the collection was to give it to the right museum. This museum was the Gardiner, because it too viewed our collection as significant and not just an accumulation of individual pieces.

Northrop Frye said that important life journeys usually end up where they started. The journey of our collection began at the Gardiner with no destination in mind and has now ended up there. When we started in 1985, we were at a point of several changes in our lives. Our objective was a new source of shared pleasure. And what a source of multiple pleasures the collection has been. Above all, collecting has been a happy shared pursuit, but it has also led to wonderful new friendships in Oxford, London, Tokyo, Kyoto, Osaka, Arita, Paris and Amsterdam. We have delighted in the objects themselves and in finding objects that would reflect the inter-influence theme. We have enjoyed the multiple experiences of Japan, with the collection providing an added focus for much of our global travel.

Lester Pearson, Canada's Nobel Peace Prize winner, told me that when you are the External Affairs Minister of Canada, you make a series of decisions and then wake up one day to find Canada has a foreign policy. We likewise made a number of individual acquisitions and woke up (thanks to Oliver Impey) to find we had a collection. Nineteen years later we moved from our home of forty-three years and awoke to the fact that this collection seemed, in the eyes of those who knew better than we, to be both worthwhile and somewhat special. We then realized that we did not want the collection to disappear. Now, in giving it to the Gardiner Museum, we have had a further, almost biblical, awakening: by giving the collection away, we somehow possess it even more than when it was still in our actual possession. One of Toronto's most generous and enthusiastic benefactors suggested that donating it makes the collection itself more than it was, perhaps because it has the added life of so many new sets of eyes to look at it.

There are two largely uncontrollable elements in the formation of any collection—what is available and, for all but the super rich, what is affordable. So our collection has been determined not just by our taste or our thinking. Omissions may be the result of either our being unable to afford some pieces or simply that such pieces have never become available. Although all significant acquisition decisions have been joint, my role has been to keep the acquisitions, for the most part, within the original two broad frames: first, seventeenth-century export polychrome Kakiemon and Kakiemon-style Japanese pieces; and second, pieces from the first ten to twenty years of the original porcelain production in Continental and English factories reflecting the Kakiemon style. Molly Anne's role has been to judge the visual and technical quality of individual pieces; the aesthetic heart of the collection has come from her. The reality of who really chose the pieces was quickly recognized by Bob Williams. To him we owe the strong English and European foundation of the collection and its initial Japanese Kakiemon base. And to Richard Barker, another London-based dealer, we owe much of the more recent stepping out from the narrower Kakiemon base to some very special (1610–70) pieces from Japan, and a few Chinese pieces in the Japanese style made for the Japanese market. When we have stepped outside the original thematic scope of the collection, it is because Molly Anne has been drawn to individual pieces, especially Shoki-Imari and Ko-Kutani.

The idea for the collection was not as intellectual as it might appear. Having bought Canadian and other art (including postwar contemporary Japanese woodblock prints) on the basis of what we liked, we wanted a stronger focus for a field as broad as porcelain. The primary focus came from Molly Anne as a result of her efforts at the Gardiner. Japan was my main focus because of important business interests. In addition, since I see Japan and the United States as constituting opposite socio-cultural extremes, Japanese society and culture became a mirror for me into the nature of the United States and of Canada. Also important was that we shared equal pleasure in so many things Japanese, from porcelain, screens and woodblock prints to traditional food and inns. We decided to focus the collection on Kakiemon and its influence in Europe for two main reasons. First, the Kakiemon pieces of the period appealed to us in a very tactile and visual way. Second, these same pieces also held great appeal to Dutch, French, German and English buyers in the late seventeenth century, and that appeal continued in their own Kakiemon-style pieces for another forty years after the Europeans had learned how to make porcelain themselves.

A few other thoughts may contribute to understanding the particular shape and content of the collection:

- We tend to prefer the earliest examples of new forms: Norman English cathedrals, thirties Hollywood films, early Group of Seven Canadian painting. Although often less refined, the early examples express more vigour and sheer delight. So for the most part, we prefer the early Shoki-Imari, the early Kakiemon and porcelain from the first few years of the European factories to examples from later, even if more refined, production.
- We bought imperfect pieces, so long as the imperfections did not jar the eye and the pieces were basically of high-quality design and enamelling. This enabled us to obtain pieces that might otherwise have been unavailable or unaffordable or unable to be exported from Japan. We learned this approach from Oliver Impey.
- In this kind of collection, which seeks to show the nature and scope of inter-influence, many pieces are bought not for their stand-alone quality but for how they contribute to the overall critical mass, or the critical mass of a particular segment. Life rarely consists of "perfect tens," and a collection of exclusively "eights," "nines" or "tens" would not only distort reality, but the absence of contrast would mask the real achievement of the makers of the best pieces.
- The collection includes a considerable number of French Samson pieces from

Fig. 3
LARGE JAR WITH DRAGON AND TIGER DESIGN
Japan, Arita, c. 1680–1700
The lid is an earthenware replacement.
The Netherlands, Delft, c. 1720–40
H: 62.2 cm

the very late nineteenth century whose quality does not match that of the Kakiemon originals or of most of the production of the main Continental and English factories. These pieces are in the collection for two reasons: many of them would have simply been unaffordable in their Japanese, Meissen or other versions; also, they allow a deeper understanding of the seventeenth-century Kakiemon achievement.

- Finally, there are English-decorated and Dutch-decorated porcelain pieces from China and Germany in the collection. These are examples of the use of outsourcing almost three centuries before it became the pervasive economic reality and political challenge it is today.

We have recently added a few examples of early seventeenth-century Chinese pieces made solely for export to Japan at the moment that Japan was making its very first porcelain in Kyushu. Thanks to Richard Barker's astonishing nose for the unusual, we have obtained not only a Chinese porcelain hexagonal export plate made for the Japanese market, but also a Japanese version of that Chinese export plate from about one hundred years later (see fig. 50). These two plates illustrate the fact that the Japanese made their own versions of Chinese export pieces created for the Japanese market, just as the Europeans did of the Kakiemon pieces, which is the precise inter-influence theme of the main collection. When comparing Japanese and European versions of the same design, the negative space, a critical design element, is almost invariably more effective in the Japanese original. In this case, the Japanese copy of the Chinese original also shows markedly better use of negative space.

Japan itself has been at the heart of both the shaping of the collection and the acquisition of many important pieces. On our first trip to Japan in 1975, we were lucky enough to find *Japanese Society,* a slim but enlightening book by Chie Nakane, an anthropologist whom I was to meet twenty years later in Tokyo. The book made clear how profound the structural difference between Japan and the West was. The challenge of that difference and our delight in that difference brought us to spend a cumulative total over the years of some fifty-two weeks in Japan. Those trips, and our porcelain collection, were essential to what I came to understand about both Japan and the West.

Molly Anne and I have been extraordinarily fortunate in our lives. Our only real goal has been to be good to each other and to raise good children. A friend at my recent eightieth birthday said he had not realized, until he saw our entire three generations and all our friends, how rich I was. What is so overwhelming for us about having a collection worth giving to the Gardiner is that it has added to an already full life the entirely unexpected opportunity to leave something behind for a larger community than that of our family. So we are overwhelmed with gratitude that our collection will live on at the Gardiner.

BILL MACDONALD

PART I

JAPANESE PORCELAIN AND ITS IMPACT IN EUROPE

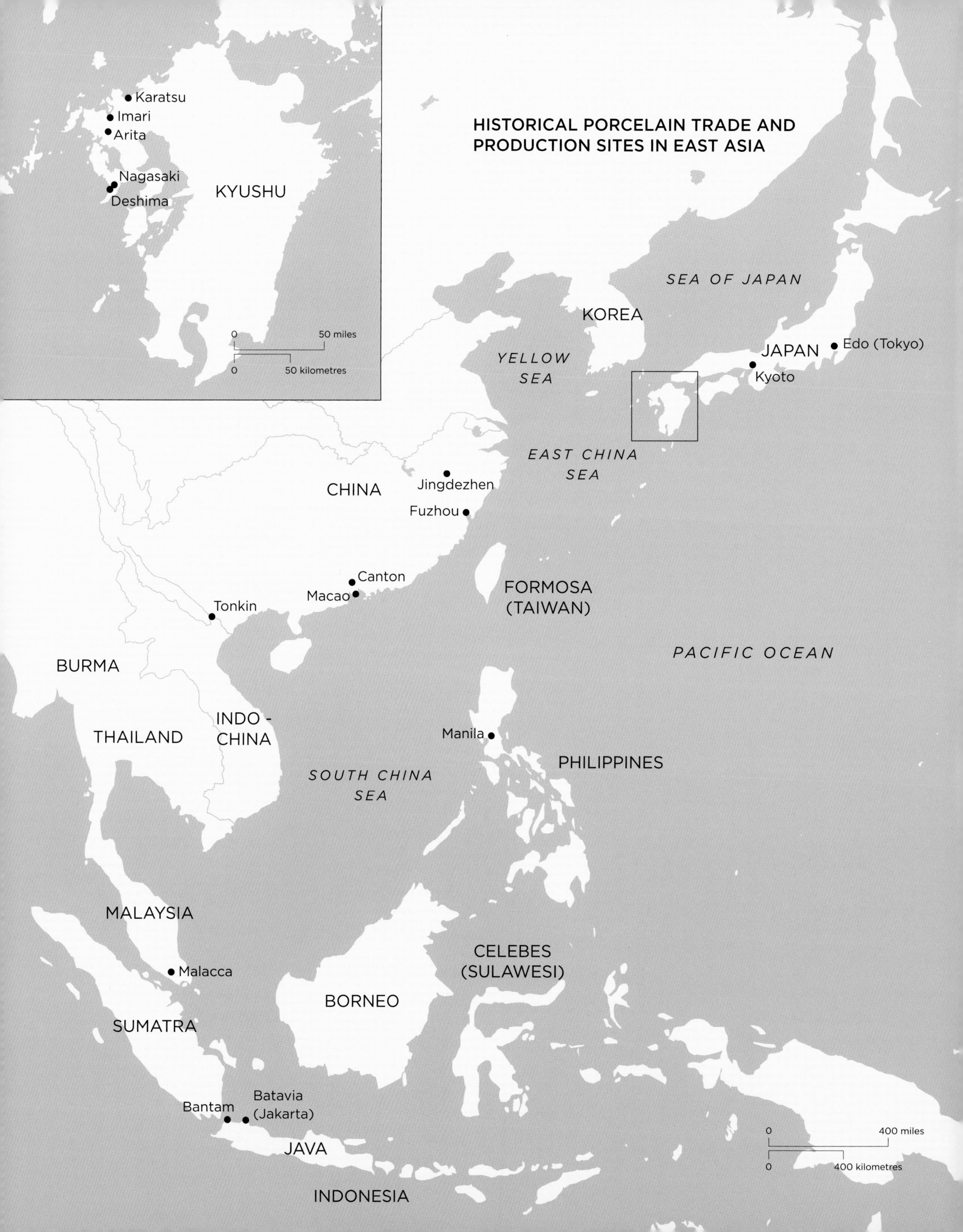
HISTORICAL PORCELAIN TRADE AND PRODUCTION SITES IN EAST ASIA
Karatsu
Imari
Arita
Nagasaki
Deshima
KYUSHU
0
50 miles
0
50 kilometres
SEA OF JAPAN
KOREA
YELLOW SEA
JAPAN
Edo (Tokyo)
Kyoto
EAST CHINA SEA
CHINA
Jingdezhen
Fuzhou
Canton
Macao
Tonkin
FORMOSA (TAIWAN)
PACIFIC OCEAN
BURMA
THAILAND
INDO - CHINA
Manila
PHILIPPINES
SOUTH CHINA SEA
MALAYSIA
Malacca
CELEBES (SULAWESI)
BORNEO
SUMATRA
Bantam
Batavia (Jakarta)
JAVA
INDONESIA
0
400 miles
0
400 kilometres

ADAPTATION AND INNOVATION: PORCELAIN IN JAPAN, 1600–1750

CHARLES MASON

PORCELAIN WAS FIRST MADE IN JAPAN sometime around 1620. Starting with a few experimental pieces that were fired together with larger batches of stoneware, the Japanese porcelain industry grew rapidly and within fifty years was producing hundreds of thousands of pieces a year. Fifty years later still, the industry went through a period of significant contraction and consolidation before beginning a new era of growth that lasted through the nineteenth and into the twentieth centuries. This essay traces the remarkable history of Japanese porcelain during the seventeenth and early eighteenth centuries and examines the important roles porcelain played in the political, economic, social and cultural life of Japan at that time.

HISTORICAL BACKGROUND

Before delving into the specific history of Japan's porcelain industry during the seventeenth and eighteenth centuries, it is necessary first to consider some of the broader historical conditions in which that industry emerged and flourished.[1]

For much of the fifteenth and sixteenth centuries, Japan was wracked by battles between opposing warlords who divided the country into numerous quasi-feudal states. In 1600, one particularly powerful warlord, Tokugawa Ieyasu, defeated his last major rival and unified the country once again. Although the emperor in Kyoto was still the nominal ruler of Japan, real political authority lay with Ieyasu, who assumed the title of shogun, or "supreme general." Ieyasu and his successors based their government in the city of Edo (modern Tokyo) and ruled with the help of an appointed administration called the *bakufu* (shogunate). The Tokugawa *bakufu* controlled the most important territories in Japan and employed the largest military force. It was responsible for maintaining order within Japan as well as for managing all of the country's foreign relations. The provincial territories not directly controlled by the Tokugawa *bakufu* were controlled by subsidiary warlords called daimyo. Although the daimyo theoretically enjoyed complete power within their domains, they were closely monitored by the Tokugawa government and were subject to various regulations devised by the *bakufu* to limit their potential for rebellion. These regulations included requirements that the daimyo attend the shogun's court in Edo for a certain period every other year, that they leave their families in Edo all year as security guarantees and that they obtain permission from the shogun to marry and to transmit their titles from generation to generation. Relations between the shogun and the daimyo were sometimes tense, but on the whole, peace prevailed and Japan enjoyed almost two and a half centuries of political stability under Tokugawa rule.

This political stability in turn enabled Japan's economy to grow and become more complex than had been possible before reunification. As relations between the central and provincial governments solidified in the seventeenth century, more roads and water transport networks were built, allowing crops and other goods to be transported more easily between different markets. The improved transportation further encouraged the producers of those crops and goods to become more efficient and to raise their production levels. The profits that accrued from trade encouraged the opening of new agricultural lands and the development of new industries such as mining, textiles and, of particular relevance here, ceramics. Money gradually replaced barter as the basis of exchange in the new economy, and the quantity and variety of goods available to consumers increased dramatically. This remarkable economic expansion faltered in the early eighteenth century as price inflation and declines in productivity led to a prolonged recessionary period between the 1710s and 1730s. Modest growth resumed again in the middle of the eighteenth century, and the economy remained fairly stable until near the end of the Tokugawa period in the 1850s and 1860s.

The radical transformation of Japan's economy during the seventeenth and eighteenth centuries was a major contributing factor to many important social changes that occurred at the same time. In theory, Japanese society during the Tokugawa period was structured according to an ancient Chinese model that grouped people into four main classes: a military-political class (samurai), an agricultural class, an artisan class and a merchant class. Status was hereditary and regulations supposedly kept each group in its place. In reality, however, Tokugawa-period society was much more complex and dynamic than the theoretical model admitted. Because the relative peacefulness of the era diminished the need for warriors, many military men were driven to become involved in art or trade. At the same time, the more commercialized nature of the economy blurred the divisions among farmers, craftsmen and merchants and produced new subgroups within each of those classes. Increasing numbers of people who did not fit into the official social structure at all, such as Buddhist monks and entertainers, further confused the situation. The resulting incongruities between the ideal and real social structures generated considerable anxiety and created a competitive social environment in which people relied heavily on outward symbols like clothing and household furnishings to define themselves and their place in the world. Because it affected people's behaviour, this more anxious and competitive social environment also had major implications for Tokugawa-period culture.

Prior to the seventeenth century, Japanese culture had been shaped primarily by the tastes of the imperial and shogunal courts in Kyoto, by the practices and patronage of Buddhist temples in the provinces and by the rhythms of daily life in the countryside. By contrast, Tokugawa-period culture came increasingly to be shaped by currents emanating from the nation's cities, especially Edo, Kyoto, Osaka and Nagasaki. These cities first emerged in the early seventeenth century as vital political and economic centres, but as they grew their impact became much broader. The dense, crowded environments in cities magnified the social tensions described above and made symbolic displays of status and identity all the more important. The fashions that were born in cities were subsequently transmitted to the nation's smaller towns and villages through another newly important cultural phenomenon, woodblock printing. Although woodblock printing was known in Japan for centuries before the Tokugawa period, it had never before been used as a form of mass communication. This changed when new printing techniques were brought from China and Korea in the early seventeenth century and put to new uses in an economic climate that made the production and distribution of printed books and images a potentially profitable business. The tremendous dissemination of information that resulted from the spread of woodblock printing vastly expanded people's intellectual horizons and changed the ways in which they interacted with each other and with their physical environment. A third important factor that contributed to the larger transformation of Japanese culture during this period was the establishment of an official system for maintaining and regulating contacts with foreign countries, primarily China, Korea and the Netherlands. This increased foreign contact combined with the effects of urbanization and the spread of knowledge through printing to produce a culture that was considerably richer, more diverse and more cosmopolitan than at any previous time in Japanese history.

The development of Japan's porcelain industry during the seventeenth and eighteenth centuries was affected by all of the historical conditions outlined above and indeed helped to shape those conditions. As will be discussed throughout this book, porcelain was involved in so many different aspects of Tokugawa-period life that it does not exaggerate to say that porcelain offers a window into the history of the entire period.

THE BEGINNINGS OF JAPAN'S PORCELAIN INDUSTRY, 1620–50

Porcelain was known in Japan long before it was made there. The first porcelains used in Japan were imported from China in the eleventh or twelfth century. These early porcelain imports included a wide range of styles and forms, from food dishes and wine flasks to vases and cosmetic boxes.[2] It is impossible to know exactly how many Chinese porcelains were imported into Japan before the seventeenth century, but quantities were certainly limited and they were expensive enough that only the highest levels of society could afford to use them.

This situation began to change in the early 1600s when a number of factors combined to bring about a dramatic rise in the number of Chinese porcelains reaching Japan. One of these factors was a decision by the Chinese government in 1567 to lift the restrictions on overseas trade that had limited Chinese access to Japanese and other foreign markets for more than a century. Eager to find fresh sources of income, Chinese merchants immediately started to export Chinese products to markets in other Asian countries. It took a few decades for this trade to become fully established, but by the end of the sixteenth century relatively large quantities of Chinese goods, including porcelains, were being shipped to Japan every year.[3] At the same time as the supply of Chinese porcelains was increasing, the above-described economic and social changes within Japan prompted a rise in demand as well and meant that more Japanese consumers had the money and desire to buy costly status symbols like Chinese porcelains.

Many of the new Japanese consumers of Chinese porcelain in the early 1600s wanted to purchase it specifically to use in the tea ceremony. Prior to the seventeenth century, the Japanese tea ceremony had been largely the preserve of

Fig. 4
FISH-SHAPED DISH
China, Jingdezhen, c. 1620–40
L: 22.5 cm

Buddhist monks and elite samurai and was dominated by an aesthetic sensibility that emphasized subtlety, understatement and rustic imperfection. In the 1590s, however, a tea master named Furuta Oribe began advocating a new style of tea ceremony that was more secular and luxurious and that expressly included the use of refined Chinese porcelains.[4] This new style of tea ceremony quickly gained popularity and attracted increasing numbers of practitioners from the lower samurai, merchant and artisan classes. The demand for porcelains to use in the tea ceremony continued under the leadership of Oribe's successor, Kobori Enshu, who further developed the ornate tea style and made it into an important component of mainstream Japanese culture.

The flow of Chinese porcelains into Japan increased substantially in the 1620s and 30s as economic problems at home forced Chinese porcelain manufacturers to seek an even greater portion of their income overseas.[5] Although many of the exported porcelains were basically the same as Chinese domestic wares, some featured special forms and designs made specifically for the Japanese market (e.g., fig. 4). The most interesting examples were based on models or images sent to China from Japan, the creation of which testifies to the economic importance of the Japanese trade at that time. But despite the best efforts of Chinese merchants to supply the Japanese market with porcelains, they could not keep up with demand, and Japanese consumers increasingly looked for domestic substitutes. Painted stoneware from Mino and Karatsu that imitated some aspects of Chinese ceramics became popular for a time in the late sixteenth and early seventeenth centuries but ultimately could not substitute for porcelain.[6] So a search began to find the right kinds of clay to make porcelain in Japan. This search was heavily informed by the knowledge and experience of Korean potters who had been brought to Japan as war captives after two Japanese invasions of the Korean peninsula in the 1590s. Many of these Korean potters were resettled on the southern island of Kyushu across the sea from their homeland, and it was there, in Hizen province (modern Saga prefecture) in the 1610s, that a Korean potter named Ri Sampei (Li Sam-py'ong) is said to have discovered suitable porcelain clays at a mountain called Izumiyama, near the town of Arita.[7]

In China, porcelain was made from a mixture of two key ingredients: china clay (kaolin), which gave the porcelain its plasticity and strength; and china stone (decayed feldspathic rock), which gave the porcelain its glassy, translucent quality. By some good fortune, the clay deposits discovered by Ri Sampei at Izumiyama contained a natural mixture of china clay and china stone, so the challenge of finding the right materials to produce porcelain in Japan was solved at one stroke. Of course, it still took some time and experimentation to figure out how to properly prepare the Izumiyama clays, how to use the prepared clays to form objects and how to fire those objects once they were formed. As was mentioned at the beginning of this essay, the first porcelains made in Japan were fired in the stoneware kilns at Karatsu. These kilns did not always burn hot enough for the porcelain to mature fully, and many early pieces came out of the kilns discoloured, warped or marred by air bubbles. It probably took several years to work through these technical problems, but by 1620 or so Japanese potters were able to produce decent-quality porcelains on a fairly consistent basis. They then established a new centre of production in the area around Arita, which was not only located near the source of the porcelain clay, but also possessed ample supplies of the water that was needed to prepare the clay and the wood that was needed to fuel the kilns. Moreover, Arita was situated only a short distance from the port town of Imari, where the finished products could be shipped off to market. And so with all the necessary components in place, a new industry was born.[8]

Unfortunately, we know very little about exactly how the Japanese porcelain industry was initially organized. Industrial porcelain production was an expensive business. It took a great deal of money and labour to mine the clay, prepare it, age it, shape it, decorate it, glaze it, fire it, pack it and ship it. Add the facts that the shaping, decorating and firing processes also required special skills that took years to master, and it is clear that the early Japanese porcelain industry must have been a very complex business. Although no records exist that describe the original structure of this business, we can imagine several possible scenarios. One scenario is that the porcelain industry was initially organized and financed by the local rulers of Hizen province, where Arita was located. Many daimyo during the seventeenth century invested in art and handicraft enterprises as a way of earning extra income for their domains, and it is difficult to imagine the local officials in Hizen not being involved in the formation of a new industry as potentially profitable as porcelain.[9] A second possible scenario is that the porcelain industry was organized and financed by consortiums of merchants and other private investors. This was the case with many Kyoto-area pottery workshops, which were backed financially by merchant clubs and Buddhist temples seeking cultural prestige as well as monetary rewards.[10] A third possible scenario is that the porcelain industry was organized and financed by individual craftsman clans. This arrangement could have happened if the clans had already amassed sufficient capital and knowledge from their participation in other ceramic industries, such as the stoneware industry at Karatsu.[11] Or a fourth possible scenario, which is perhaps the most likely, is that the porcelain industry was initially organized and financed by a combination of different elements, with some workshops being backed by provincial authorities, some by mercantile investors and some by the craftsman families themselves.

The most skilled jobs in the porcelain industry—potting, decorating and kiln operation—were almost certainly controlled by families that passed their knowledge on from generation to generation as a kind of trade secret. As Oliver Impey's essay in this book discusses, the famous Kakiemon style may have begun with the products of one such family-run workshop. When the porcelain industry was still in its infancy, these workshops may have been rather small affairs with just a few people performing most of the tasks. But as the industry developed, the various stages in the production process probably became more specialized and the number of people involved more numerous. Indeed, one indication of just how quickly the Japanese porcelain industry grew in its first few decades is a 1637 document from the Hizen provincial government ordering 826 workers in the industry to leave their new jobs and return to their original occupations.[12] If 826 people could be removed from the workforce and the industry still continue to function, it must have been a large and well-organized industry already by that time.

Because Japan's porcelain industry evolved at least partly in response to a demand for Chinese wares, it should come as no surprise that the forms and decoration of the earliest Japanese porcelains mainly follow Chinese models, with some Korean inflections. The most common forms produced during the industry's early years were small food dishes, bowls, sake bottles and incense burners. This range of forms was determined partly by consumer demand for certain functions and partly by the limits of the available technology. When the porcelain industry was newly established, Japanese potters were still using relatively simple kilns and firing techniques, and they did not have the capacity to fire many large pieces.[13] Early Japanese porcelains were often a bit crude, but they were closer to Chinese porcelains than any other Japanese ceramics, and as their quality improved over time, the Japanese porcelains became more than adequate replacements for the Chinese wares that originally inspired them.

The decoration on early Japanese porcelains consisted mainly of plain moulded or blue painted designs on a white body beneath a clear glaze. These two types of decoration dominated Japanese porcelain production for the first two decades of the industry's existence. Then, sometime around the 1640s, Japanese potters developed new techniques for decorating porcelains with enamel colours that were applied over the glaze and fixed with a separate firing. The materials and techniques needed to produce this type of overglaze enamel decoration may have been brought to Japan by Chinese potters fleeing political turmoil in their homeland.[14] These refugees may also have brought other knowledge about clay preparation and firing techniques, since there seems to have been a sudden increase in the overall quality of Japanese porcelains at about the same time. But although the overglaze enamelling technique may originally have come from China, Japanese potters soon adapted it to suit their own artistic ends. One example of this adaptation was the development of an overglaze cobalt-blue enamel that was not used in China but became common in Japan. The introduction of enamelling to Japan greatly increased the attractiveness of Japanese porcelains and allowed them to compete more successfully with other types of Japanese ceramics being produced at the same time. Furthermore, the addition of enamelled wares to the product lines also set the stage for the entry of foreign buyers into the Japanese market, which would profoundly change the entire industry.

THE INDUSTRY EXPANDS, 1650–1700

The first Japanese porcelains were made exclusively for the domestic market and were purchased mainly by elite samurai, wealthy merchants, affluent artisans and higher-ranking Buddhist monks. As the quality of Japanese porcelain gradually improved between the 1620s and 1640s, demand increased as well, but the production volume probably still remained rather low until the 1650s, when a number of forces combined to drive a rapid expansion of the porcelain industry. One of these forces was the growing popularity of the tea ceremony, as has already been discussed. A second force was the introduction of regulations requiring the provincial daimyo to maintain second residences in the city of Edo.[15] Once built, these lavish residences had to be furnished, and this in turn created a significant new demand for porcelains. The growth of cities in general was a third force encouraging demand for Japanese porcelains. Along with the daimyo, many other classes were also building new houses and including porcelains among their furnishings.[16] But perhaps the biggest factor driving the increased demand for domestic porcelain in Japan during the 1650s was a sharp decrease in supplies of porcelain from China. As was discussed above, China produced large quantities of porcelain for the Japanese market in the 1620s and 30s. This porcelain competed with the domestically produced porcelain and undercut its production during those decades. Then, in 1644, the Ming dynasty in China collapsed and several years of fighting ensued as various factions battled to form a new dynasty. Exports of porcelain from China rapidly dwindled as production at Jingdezhen decreased and trading networks were disrupted by the turmoil of the dynastic transition. Without competition from Chinese porcelains, the Japanese industry quickly ramped up its own production to fill the supply void and meet the increasing domestic demand.[17]

The decline in Chinese porcelain exports in the mid-seventeenth century drove the demand for Japanese porcelain, both from within Japan and from Europe. Demand for porcelain was huge in Europe and other parts of the world during the seventeenth century. European merchants had been feeding that demand with porcelains from China for many decades.[18] When Chinese porcelains suddenly became more difficult to obtain, European merchants looked for a substitute source of supply and soon settled on Japan. Japanese porcelain was attractive to European traders for a number of reasons. For one thing, the Japanese potters were very familiar with Chinese forms and styles and could produce passable imitations of Chinese wares if requested. Moreover, the Japanese industry was already well developed and was conveniently located close to established trading routes. One impediment to an expanded porcelain trade between Japan and Europe was a "closed door" *(sakoku)* policy imposed by the Tokugawa government in 1639 to keep out Christian missionaries. This policy allowed only Chinese, Korean and Dutch merchants to trade directly with the Japanese. But with those merchants taking Japanese porcelains to markets elsewhere in Asia and Europe and reselling them, Japanese porcelains soon became part of a much larger, global business network.

The first Japanese porcelains purchased by the Dutch in 1650 consisted of 145 "coarse dishes" that were taken to be resold in the markets of Tonkin (Vietnam).[19] The Dutch gradually increased their orders over the next few years as they tested other markets for Japanese porcelain in Europe, the Middle East and Southeast Asia. Finally convinced of Japanese porcelain's potential profitability, the Dutch dramatically increased their order in 1659 to almost 57,000 pieces. This order seems to have taken the Japanese potters by surprise, and it took them two years to completely fill the shipment. The Dutch continued to place large orders for Japanese porcelain throughout the 1660s, 70s and 80s. At the same time, Chinese merchants also began to buy significant quantities of Japanese porcelains for resale to European merchants in other markets. The size of the Chinese orders is more difficult to quantify, but it was probably at least as great as the Dutch orders and possibly greater. Thus, between its domestic and foreign customers, the Japanese porcelain industry had to contend with a rapid increase in demand, from perhaps tens of thousands of pieces per year to hundreds of thousands. To cope with the new level of demand, the porcelain industry in Arita underwent significant reorganization in the 1660s.[20] More kilns were built. The different stages of the production process became more specialized. The delivery infrastructure was improved. And perhaps most importantly, new decorative styles emerged as potters sought to create more distinctive products that would meet the different tastes of their expanding consumer base.

The first distinct decorative style to emerge in the late 1640s and 50s was the Ko-Kutani style.[21] Heavily inspired by Chinese models, this style was characterized by the use of rich enamel colours and bold patterns. Ko-Kutani wares were made primarily for the domestic market, though some were also exported to Southeast Asia. A second major style that evolved in the 1660s and 70s was the Kakiemon style.[22] Kakiemon porcelains were decorated with more translucent enamels and typically featured asymmetrical designs placed against generous expanses of blank ground. The Kakiemon style may have been the first to evolve in response to both domestic and foreign demand, and

Fig. 5
KAKIEMON BOWL WITH DRAGON MEDALLION
Japan, Arita, c. 1700–10
D: 22 cm

it quickly became an important force in the entire industry. A third major style that also evolved in the 1670s was the Imari style.[23] The Imari style featured a darker enamel palette that was often enhanced by gilding. Compared with the Kakiemon style, Imari designs were much denser and more symmetrical. They were also typically less pictorial than either Ko-Kutani or Kakiemon wares. Like Kakiemon, Imari ware was enjoyed by both domestic and foreign consumers, though in slightly different versions.

Ko-Kutani, Kakiemon and Imari became the dominant commercial styles of Japanese porcelain in the second half of the seventeenth century. In addition to these commercial wares, two non-commercial wares also emerged that enjoyed limited circulation within the Japanese domestic market exclusively. The first of these was Nabeshima ware.[24] Nabeshima was the surname of the daimyo family that ruled Hizen. Because Nabeshima forces had fought against the Tokugawa clan in the civil wars leading up to reunification, relations between the Nabeshima daimyos and the Tokugawa shoguns were somewhat uneasy. To demonstrate their respect for and allegiance to the Tokugawa clan, the early seventeenth-century Nabeshima daimyos regularly sent gifts of Chinese, and later, Arita porcelains to Edo. As the porcelain industry expanded in response to increasing domestic and foreign demand in the 1650s and 60s, the Nabeshima rulers grew concerned that they would not always be able to obtain high-quality wares of the types they needed for their tribute porcelains, so they established their own private porcelain factory near the village of Okawachi, not far from Arita. The Nabeshima factory was staffed with some of the best workers drawn from the commercial factories in Arita and produced highly refined, richly coloured wares that were heavily influenced by contemporary textile and lacquer designs. Its wares were not for sale and were requisitioned by the Nabeshima clan for its own use or for use as gifts to the emperor, shogun and various important allies.

The second non-commercial type of porcelain to emerge in the seventeenth century was Hirado ware.[25] Hirado ware was named after an island off the coast of Kyushu where the Matsuura daimyo clan was based. The Matsuura domain also included territory on Kyushu where deposits of suitable porcelain clay were discovered sometime around the 1630s. Inspired by the growing success of the porcelain industry in nearby Arita, the Matsuura daimyo founded a porcelain workshop in the village of Mikawachi to make wares for his own private uses. This workshop was small, and because its products did not circulate widely, it did not have as much of an impact on Japanese or European cultures as did the Arita wares during the seventeenth and eighteenth centuries. But Hirado wares were known in Japanese aristocratic circles. There are records of Hirado porcelains being presented to the shogun in 1664 and to the emperor in 1699. And when the Matsuura daimyo stopped supporting Hirado financially in the early nineteenth century and turned it into a commercial enterprise, its wares did finally filter out to ordinary consumers in both Japan and the West.

The impact that the expansion of Japan's porcelain industry had on Europe is discussed in Christiaan Jörg's essay and other sections of this book. The focus here is the impact that this expansion had on Japanese domestic culture in the late seventeenth and early eighteenth centuries. As production levels rose and various styles emerged, porcelains quickly became an important part of Japan's physical environment. Confirmation of how extensive the use of porcelain became can be found in archaeological evidence from the period. Excavations of the remains of daimyo and other elite residences from the seventeenth and eighteenth centuries reveal large quantities of porcelain shards, usually mixed together with other kinds of ceramics. For example, excavations in Tokyo of the site once occupied by the residence of the Matsudaira daimyo from the Takamatsu domain recovered some 30,300 ceramic shards. Of these shards, 26 per cent were porcelain, 61 per cent were stoneware and 12 per cent were earthenware.[26] The shards came from a wide variety of forms, including dishes, bowls, flasks and cups, and demonstrate that porcelain was thoroughly integrated into the domestic environment of that time.

Additional evidence for the widespread use of porcelain in Japan in the late seventeenth and early eighteenth centuries can be found in contemporary paintings, especially paintings from the emerging Ukiyo-e school that chronicled the pleasurable activities of urban life. One early Ukiyo-e artist in particular, whose works often depict people using porcelains, is Miyagawa Choshun (1682–1752). His corpus of work includes a number of screen and scroll paintings that show people at banquets and other festive gatherings using both blue-and-white and polychrome-enamel porcelains in combination with a wide variety of other objects made from lacquer, metal and non-porcelain ceramic.[27] Although these images were not created to be chronicles of daily life as such, they expand our understanding of the different contexts in which porcelains were used and how they were integrated into other aspects of the material environment at the time.

A final source of evidence for the increasingly central role of porcelains in Japanese culture during the late seventeenth and eighteenth centuries is the objects themselves. As will be discussed throughout this book, Japanese porcelains overlapped considerably with other types of art such as paintings, prints, lacquers and textiles. Many of the decorative motifs that were used on porcelains had either symbolic meanings or literary associations that would have resonated strongly in the popular culture of the period. These connections to other arts and to popular culture prove that porcelain was engaged in a much larger artistic and cultural dialogue and that it was no longer confined to the periphery of Japanese culture as it had been before 1600.

CONTRACTION AND CONSOLIDATION, 1700–50

After growing rapidly in the second half of the seventeenth century, Japan's porcelain industry ran into a number of difficulties in the first few decades of the eighteenth century. One of these difficulties was a period of economic depression in Japan during the 1710s and 20s caused by runaway inflation and declining productivity in Japan's mining and agricultural sectors.[28] The economic downturn prompted the Tokugawa government to impose new sumptuary laws regulating the types of luxury goods people could produce and use. These regulations, coupled with the fact that many consumers had less money available to spend, dampened the demand for porcelain in Japan. At the same time, China's porcelain industry re-emerged as a major supplier of porcelains to the markets in Europe and elsewhere around the world. The Chinese were very aware of how Japan had stepped into the export market in the 1650s and 60s, and they attempted to undermine the Japanese porcelain industry by imitating their wares and undercutting their prices.[29] Lured back by the Chinese, Western demand for Japanese porcelains soon began to drop and dipped even further after potters in Europe discovered the secret of porcelain production for themselves.

The combination of reduced domestic and foreign demand thus forced a severe contraction of the porcelain industry in Arita during the 1720s and 30s. Some sense of how difficult the situation became is provided by a 1723 letter from the head of the Kakiemon family to the Nabeshima daimyo:

> We have been practising the trade for generations, but there are no special orders during the present year and the trade has decreased year by year. Therefore, our workmen—potters and painters—have nothing to do, to say nothing of myself, and our poverty increases day by day.[30]

As their customer base diminished, many workshops and kilns went out of business. Production volumes fell, styles ossified or were temporarily interrupted, and the overall quality and variety of the wares being produced declined from the high points of the seventeenth century. In many ways it was the end of

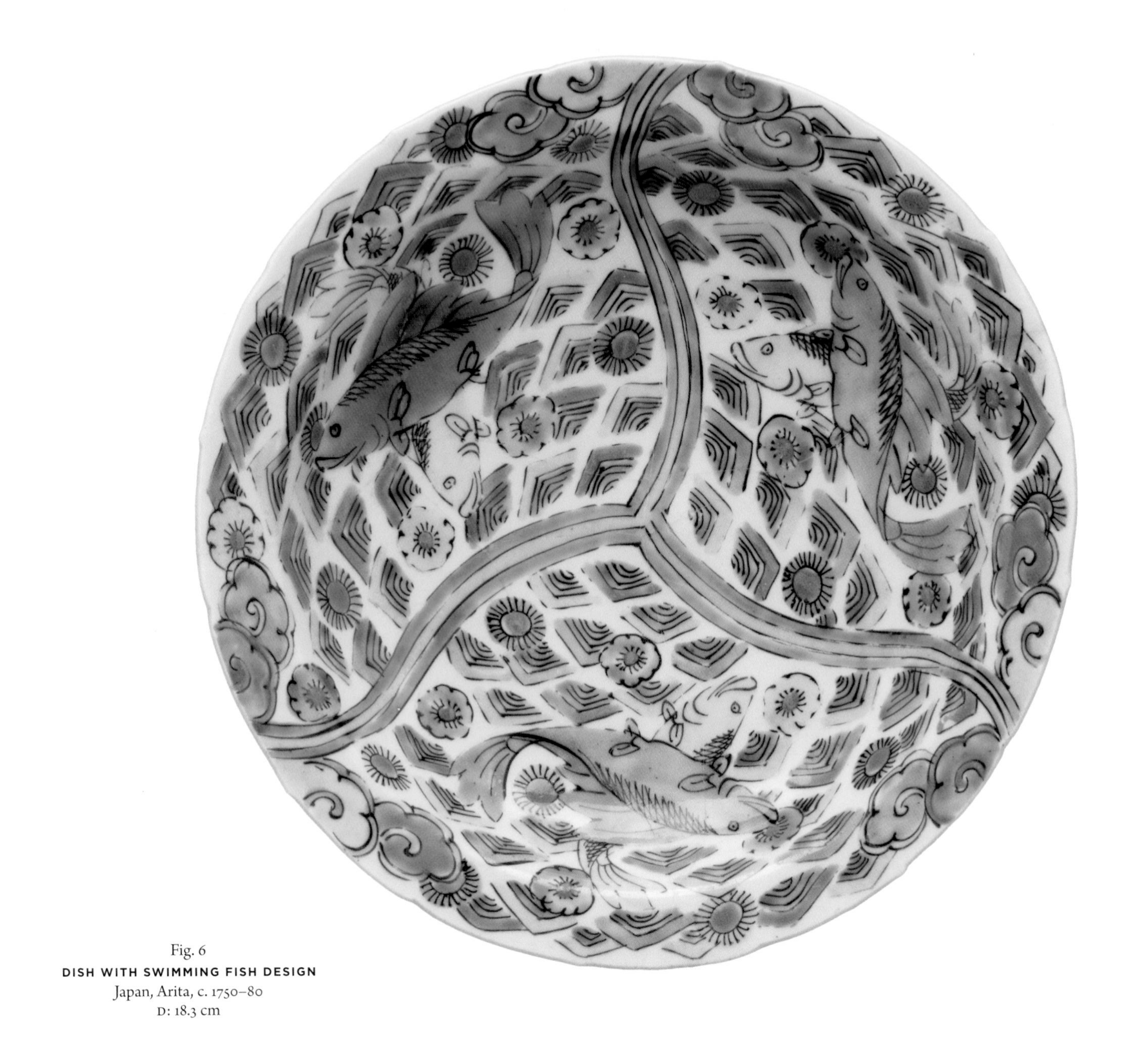

Fig. 6
DISH WITH SWIMMING FISH DESIGN
Japan, Arita, c. 1750–80
D: 18.3 cm

an era and thus is a fitting point at which to conclude this essay. But the end of the story told here does not mean that the story of Japanese porcelain itself came to an end in the first half of the eighteenth century. Quite to the contrary, after Japan's economy recovered in the 1750s, the porcelain industry in Arita enjoyed a new period of growth during which porcelain became even further integrated into mainstream Japanese culture. What is more, porcelain also began to be made in several other locations around Japan, creating a more stable base for the industry and preparing the way for porcelain to become the dominant type of ceramic in Japan during the twentieth century.

THE ORIGINS AND EVOLUTION OF KAKIEMON

OLIVER IMPEY

This essay is an abridged version of a lecture presented to the Oriental Ceramic Society/Christie's Annual Lecture at Christie's London on November 9, 2003. The original essay was published in *Transactions of the Oriental Ceramic Society*, Vol. 68 (2003–2004). It is reproduced here with the kind permission of the Oriental Ceramic Society.

Fig. 7
KAKIEMON BOWL WITH SEASONAL FLOWERS
Japan, Arita, c. 1670–90
D: 21.3 cm G05.11.13

KAKIEMON IS THE HONORIFIC NAME given to the senior member of the Sakaida family of the Nangawara kiln, which lies just outside Arita, a town in Saga prefecture on Kyushu, the southernmost of the four main islands of Japan.[1] The successive kilns at Nangawara have become known as the Kakiemon kiln; this name is correct for the position today, but in the seventeenth and eighteenth centuries the kilns were used by several distinct workshops of potters, of which the Kakiemon were one, possibly the major one.

The word Kakiemon also describes a style of porcelain that bears a variety of usually pictorial patterns in a style of painting that can be distinguished from other styles (with some caveats described below), often in a particular palette of enamel colours (e.g., fig. 56), or in blue and white alone (fig. 80), or a combination of the two (fig. 79). This latter part of the definition of course raises several questions. First, it does not describe any evolution either toward the style or toward the palette. Second, it postulates no origin for the porcelain. Third, any suggestion of origin does not distinguish among the potters' workshops that shaped the pieces and applied the underglaze blue, where present, and the unfired glaze; the high-temperature kilns where the pots were fired; or the workshops in which the pieces that were to be enamelled were decorated and refired at a low temperature.

There are further problems. Certainly much of the production of the porcelain we recognize as Kakiemon was made at the Nangawara site, as excavation and surface finds demonstrate. But not only was much of it evidently not made at the site (lack of shards), but also much porcelain that is clearly unrelated to the Kakiemon style was fired at the Nangawara kilns. These pieces must have been made at other potteries that used certain chambers of the Nangawara kilns concurrently with the Kakiemon potters.

The pieces of so-called Kakiemon that were not made at the site fall into three categories. First, there are those that predate the foundation of the first of the Nangawara kilns, as revealed by excavation, and belong to the somewhat catch-all category of Early Enamelled Ware, of which one subgroup appears to be ancestral to the Kakiemon (e.g., fig. 8). The second category comprises closed shapes such as bottles and jars (e.g., fig. 72), none of which are present as shard material at the kiln sites. The third category is of wares found at other kiln sites in Arita that closely resemble pieces found at the Nangawara site; these pieces must be the work of imitators or competitors (see below). Ornamental figures, a specialized product, will also be discussed below.

The Nangawara kiln sites are well known and have been excavated,[2] but the excavation led to an error in the classification of the found material. Everything found at the site has been called Kakiemon, whereas much of the material is manifestly different, quite unrelated to what is usually called Kakiemon in style and decoration. This error has only recently been identified.[3] Furthermore, the only shards found at kiln sites, namely the sites of the high-firing *noborigama* "climbing kilns," are blue and white, white, celadon, monochrome blue *(ruri)*, iron brown and, in rare cases, copper red (not found at Nangawara), or any combination of these. These colours are all first-firing colours, capable of withstanding the high temperature required for the maturation of the Arita body and clay: 1,280 degrees Celsius. Enamelled shards are almost never found at *noborigama* sites. No enamelling workshop or low-firing kiln has been found anywhere in the Arita area; we do not know even what shape these (presumably muffle) kilns were, let alone where they were or what relationship they had with the high-firing kilns. Thus we do not know where or exactly how any Kakiemon porcelain was enamelled (but see below for some discussion of this and of the ornamental figures found at the "post office site").

We do not know how the kilns of Arita stood in relationship to each other. Although they were under the rule of the Nabeshima *han* (domain) through the intermediary of the Sarayama Daikan (a local administrator) and members of the Taku family, it is not known whether the workshops and kilns competed with each other or collaborated, whether the orders were distributed among the kilns or were solicited by each kiln.[4] The products of some kilns may even have been speculative, simply for sale. During the official export period (from 1659 to 1683; after this date almost all trade was licensed private trade), Dutch records state that the potters visited the Dutch to receive their order for the year, but whether these potters were truly kiln masters or workshop masters

Fig. 8
CYLINDRICAL BOWL
Japan, Arita, c. 1660
D: 11.1 cm

or were entrepreneurs and intermediaries is not known.[5] Before the export period, there were clearly different categories of kilns distinguished by the style or quality of their products and sometimes even by their geographical area. But during the export period (during which the Nangawara kiln was founded), the ten or so kilns providing export wares did not vary all that much except, apparently, in size.[6] The sole exception is the first Nangawara kiln, probably the only kiln specifically built to produce wares for export, as opposed to being an existing kiln adapted to do so; the reasons for this will be discussed below. The Nangawara kilns may have received orders directly from the Chinese (see below); if so, this case may be an exception.

THE KAKIEMON FAMILY: HISTORY AND LEGENDS

Just as the origin of the making of porcelain in Japan is attributed to Ri Sampei,[7] so the origin of the use of enamel overglaze colours is attributed to Sakaida Kakiemon.[8] There is no contemporary evidence, however, for either of these stories. Although Ri Sampei is a known historical figure, nothing connects him in any way with the porcelain industry of Arita.[9] The existence of a Sakaida Kakiemon in the mid-seventeenth century is doubted, and there is no real evidence of how the technique of enamelling was introduced to Arita. In the first case, the porcelain that was initially produced in Japan in the first or second decade of the century was simply an extension of the existing Karatsu stoneware production; in the second case, the technique of enamelling on glazed pottery was possibly either introduced from Kyoto[10] or was imitated from Chinese wares, probably in the 1640s. Neither explanation is certain; the early Arita enamels do not resemble the early Kyoto enamels, and the early Arita enamelled wares use an overglaze cobalt blue not known in China.[11] The questions remain.

Jenyns in 1965 printed the traditional family tree of the successive Kakiemons from the first, said to have been born in 1596, to Kakiemon XI, who died in 1917. Jenyns was not without some skepticism.[12] The present author, while skeptical of all details, considers that some of the legends may be based on fact.

A series of documents preserved in the Sakaida family has been cited as evidence of the family's antiquity and as evidence of their pre-eminent place in the history of the production of, particularly, enamelled wares in Arita. These documents have provoked much discussion, and it is prudent here to follow Nishida, with reservations.[13]

Nishida discusses five documents belonging to the Sakaida family. The first is an undated letter from a priest of the Shotenji temple to Sakaida Ensei (supposedly the father of Sakaida Kakiemon I), introducing one Takahara Goroshichi; Nishida describes this letter as a fake. The second, third and fourth are interrelated; the undated second document is signed by Kizaemon (who is said possibly to have been Kakiemon I), claiming the invention of both enamelling and of colouring in gold and silver. The third is signed by Sakaida Kakiemon (supposedly Kakiemon III) and is a petition to the fief, asking for special favours in view of his father's invention of the enamelling technique; it mentions, "our porcelain trade met many difficulties, because the market price became extremely low. Finally, we had to give up the trade for a while as we could not find buyers for all our fine porcelain with elaborate decoration."[14] The fourth is unsigned but dated 1723 and says much the same as the third document. The fifth document is a certificate dated 1685 supposedly granting privileges to the Sakaida family. Nishida disbelieves the authenticity of document five and doubts numbers two, three and four. For reasons that will be discussed below, the present writer is now inclined to believe the possible authenticity of numbers three and four, purely on their content.[15]

The Sakaida family owns some one thousand moulds for vessels of various shapes and dates, some of which bear the name Sakaida and some of which are dated.[16] Dated moulds run from the Empo period (1673–81) to 1815. The earliest dated mould to bear a name is for a bowl, and the mould is signed "Nangawara-yama Tanaka Shinsaburo" and dated 1689; a blue and white bowl decorated in the Kakiemon style that appears to have been pulled from this mould was exhibited in 2002.[17] No mould with both the Sakaida name and a date is earlier than 1715. Many of the later moulds in no way resemble the Kakiemon style, though some are marked "Toshiki-yama," which is another name for Nangawara but may refer to Nangawara-Kamanotsuji.

THE NANGAWARA KILNS

Excavations in 1978 and 1979 revealed two successive kilns on the Nangawara site. No trace of any workshop was found. The present Kakiemon factory is in the valley, well below the kiln sites. The earlier kiln of the two (called kiln B) seems to have been in use for the main period of production, followed by kiln A. Kiln B could not be fully excavated but consisted of at least eighteen chambers, about 69 metres long, on a slope of 14.5 degrees. This size was fairly standard for a kiln of the period.[18]

Judging from the shards found at the site (which came inextricably mixed from both kilns), the starting date must have been in the late 1670s and the cessation probably in the 1720s. Shards of blue and white were the commonest, but white wares, including the famous *nigoshide,* were found, and pieces intended for enamelling, including blue and white that allowed for any enamel decoration as well as blue and white that demanded specific decoration; celadon wares and monochrome blue were also included in the shards. As mentioned above, no closed shapes were found, only bowls, cups, plates and shaped dishes. Many of the shapes were familiar from European collections. Shards of work of other porcelain factories were also present (see above).

ORNAMENTAL FIGURES

In 1986 and 1987, on the site of the former post office, excavations of the Aka-e-machi, the area in which the enamel kilns were said to be, and where, officially, all enamelling took place, revealed some striking evidence.[19] The site is flat and therefore could not have had a *noborigama* on it, and yet there was a quantity of kiln furniture found, suggesting the presence of nearby muffle kilns that used kiln furniture. Shards of enamelled ware (almost never found at *noborigama*), shards of pieces waiting to be enamelled (that is, glazed and high-fired) and shards of some biscuit figures were found, together with some enamelled shards, suggesting both a porcelain workshop and the rubbish dump of an enamelling kiln. Also found were press-moulds for ornamental figures, some certainly intended for Kakiemon enamels, and press-moulds for modelled dishes.[20] These finds suggest that figures and some other complex shapes, uniquely, would have been made in the Aka-e-machi, biscuit-fired before being sent to a *noborigama* and returned to the Aka-e-machi to be enamelled. Almost no biscuit shards are found at seventeenth- and early eighteenth-century Arita *noborigama* sites, from which we deduce that everything (other than these types) was raw-glazed; if there had been a biscuit firing, literally tons of biscuit shards would have been found. There is no evidence that, as is usually stated, the Kakiemon were privileged by being allowed to enamel porcelains outside the Aka-e-machi.

NIGOSHIDE

The famous milk-white body that is characteristic of one type of Kakiemon product was certainly fired in the Kakiemon kilns, as quantities of *nigoshide* shard material attest. Some moulded patterns conform to types known in European collections. This body, the whitest Oriental porcelain body other than that of Dehua *(blanc-de-Chine)*, is more refined than other Arita bodies; it never bears underglaze blue. Kakiemon XIII told the present writer that it was not from a different source but was simply more levigated than other Izumiyama bodies, which seems quite plausible.[21] Blue and white decoration was never used on Kakiemon wares with the *nigoshide* body.

THE EXPORT TRADE AND THE EVOLUTION OF THE KAKIEMON STYLE

The Dutch East India Company was the only European company with access to Japan between 1639 and the mid-nineteenth century.[22] This monopoly was always shared with the Chinese. The first purchases by the Dutch, recorded in 1650, were pieces for use rather than for resale.[23] In 1658 an order for blue and white for Southeast Asia was accompanied by an order for some six thousand sample pieces for Europe, most of which were enamelled. This order was presumably made because the Dutch were unable to order porcelain in shapes they wanted from Jingdezhen, which was then being fought over. The Dutch merchants in Japan must have been aware of the high quality of the Arita enamel colours and wanted to see if they would find favour with their masters in Amsterdam.

Enamelling seems to have begun in Arita in the 1640s, and enamelled wares were certainly exported in 1658;[24] gold and silver were added at approximately the same time, certainly by 1659.[25] The earliest dateable inventoried enamelled pieces in Europe, those at Burghley House, include a figure that may well have been one of the 295 "small statuettes on tortoises" imported in 1665;[26] this piece of Early Enamelled Ware is decorated with a palette of enamels that might be called proto-Kakiemon.[27] This palette is quite distinct from several identifiable others. Clearly, the Kakiemon, whoever they were, were enamellers before the Nangawara kiln was set up.[28] There are numerous pieces known in this palette and in the slight improvements of this palette that seem to have occurred in time. Also at Burghley, and inventoried in 1688, is a mug that bears colours marginally better, meaning clearer and brighter, than those on the tortoise, as well as a pair of figures of elephants, from the same inventory, where the Kakiemon colours are fully developed.[29] The difference in colouring must mean that the mug is earlier, probably made in the 1670s, and that the elephants would likely be from around 1680. The Kakiemon palette was established by 1688 and almost certainly earlier. The Nangawara B kiln was built around this time and was probably set up to exploit the *nigoshide* body, which showed these fine enamels to best advantage. The palette of enamels contains colours that are clear and transparent, chiefly yellow, blue and green. The red was always opaque, and aubergine, common on Imari wares, is rarely, if ever, used. Gold decoration was used very sparingly. Black was used chiefly for somewhat vague outlining but also occasionally for actual painting.

The Kakiemon appear to have continued to be enamellers of work made at other workshops and kilns at the same time as the Nangawara kilns were in production; this arrangement we have discussed above when we noticed the lack of shards of closed shapes at the Nangawara kilns. Closed shapes, particularly jars of various sizes and bottles, comprise a considerable proportion of known Kakiemon wares.

Other enamelling workshops of the 1670s to 1690s used palettes of enamels that closely resemble those of the Kakiemon but yet seem distinct. For instance, the famous "jars of six squares" of the Kensington Palace inventory of 1693 bear an enamel brown, found only on a few other shapes, notably the square-sided jars resembling Dutch gin bottles.[30] Surely, if the Kakiemon had had the enamel brown, it would appear frequently on other shapes.

The *nigoshide* body has also been found at other kiln sites, notably Kusunokidani, suggesting commercial competition.[31] That this competition may have failed is suggested by the very rarity of the shards at the sites. An iron-brown edge characterizes many of the higher-quality pieces, especially those in *nigoshide* (e.g., fig. 64), but this is neither universal for the products of the Nangawara kilns nor confined to those kilns only.

The painting style of the Kakiemon of course evolved over time, but it was always somewhat sparse in comparison with the Imari wares and more delicate. (Imari wares, which are not considered here, were far more numerous than Kakiemon wares.) The borders tend to become less marked or to disappear (e.g., fig. 65). Animals and flowers and birds are the most common motifs; occasionally there is pure pattern (e.g., fig. 2). Human figures are sometimes depicted, most famously in the "Hob in the Well" pattern that illustrates a Chinese folk tale (fig. 69) and in the "Lady on the Veranda" or "Old Lady" pattern (fig. 70). The high quality of the decoration is equally evident in the Kakiemon blue and white (e.g., figs. 81 and 82).

As with the Imari, ornamental figures are found in Kakiemon colours. The most frequently found figures are the *bijin,* or beautiful woman figure, of which there are several minor variants (e.g., figs. 60 and 61), and other human models. But there are also many other figures, such as *shishi* (lion dogs), dragons, elephants, ducks and fish. These tend to be carefully modelled after the casting in press-moulds, such as those found in the Aka-e-machi.

THE EXPORT OF KAKIEMON PORCELAIN

The lack of Kakiemon porcelain in old Dutch collections and its omnipresence in British, French and German collections has led to the suggestion that the Kakiemon porcelain was sold to the Chinese, rather than to the Dutch, for resale in Eastern ports to those European nations that had a presence in the East but no access to Japan.[32] It is known that the Chinese bought Japanese porcelain for export in the late seventeenth century, presumably at least in part because of the turmoil at Jingdezhen and elsewhere concomitant with the civil wars that led to the fall of the Ming dynasty and the rise of the Qing. Furthermore, the very fact that we distinguish the Kakiemon from the Imari wares suggests a different market. If this distinction were so, it would explain the quiet, understated style of the Kakiemon, fully in accord with Chinese taste and dissimilar to the baroque overdecoration demanded by the Dutch.

THE END OF THE KAKIEMON

It has been estimated, purely on stylistic grounds, that the Nangawara kilns ceased production in the 1720s and possibly were revived later, or at least imitated later. This date seems probable, as it was at about this time that the

Chinese ceased to buy Japanese porcelain for export. At least some other export kilns continued production of blue and white and of polychrome enamelled Imari wares considerably later than this, though the major trade with the Dutch ceased in about 1740, probably because of price wars with China.

Two additional pieces of evidence suggest this date is accurate. First, if we accept the authenticity of documents three and four in the Sakaida family archives, they would indicate that the Kakiemon were unable to sell their porcelain around 1723, which fits in with the suggested timing of the withdrawal of custom by the Chinese. Second, the celebrated case of Rodolphe Lemaire, who attempted in 1728 to have the Meissen factory make imitations of Kakiemon porcelains without the factory mark, a clear indication of an attempt to pass the copies off as originals, makes it seem more than likely that the originals were no longer available rather than merely expensive.[33]

Kakiemon-style pieces of lesser quality, with weak drawing and indifferent colouration and which use patterns associated with the 1730s rather than the 1720s, are also well known, though they are by no means always recognized. These pieces suggest a short-lived revival, and shards of such pieces have been found at the Kamanotsuji kiln site, also in the Nangawara valley.[34]

That the Kakiemon continued to make porcelain for the domestic market until at least well into the nineteenth century is evident by the existence of the late moulds, marked Sakaida, referred to above. One would be excused for failing to recognize the actual pieces as products of the Kakiemon.[35]

The Kakiemon style remained popular in Europe long after its production and importation ceased. The wares of Chantilly and Meissen may have been contemporary with the last phase of Kakiemon and have sometimes been suggested as commercial rivals, though this seems unlikely. But later factories also specialized in imitations and pastiches of the Kakiemon style, especially in England at Chelsea, Bow and Worcester, but also at Meissen, Chantilly, Saint-Cloud and many other factories. These factories were certainly commercially successful for a major part of the eighteenth century.[36]

The Sakaida family seems to have had a revival in the nineteenth century, when the old style became popular again, and today has a large workshop and a wood-fired kiln in the valley of Nangawara; the present Kakiemon XIV is a *ningen kokuho* (living national treasure). The legacy of this lovely porcelain continues to the present day.

"THE COLOURS OF OLD JAPAN": JAPANESE EXPORT PORCELAIN, KAKIEMON AND EUROPEAN IMITATIONS

CHRISTIAAN J.A. JÖRG

Fig. 9
KAKIEMON DISH WITH DRAGON AND TIGER
Japan, Arita, c. 1670–90
D: 23 cm

Fig. 10
PLATE WITH DRAGON AND FOX
The Netherlands, Delft, c. 1720–40
D: 23 cm

EVEN BEFORE the Dutch East India Company (Verenigde Oost-Indische Compagnie or VOC) was founded in 1602, the Dutch ship *De Liefde* had reached the shores of Kyushu by chance in 1600. The Dutch-Japanese relationship, based solely on the profits of mutual trade, became even more exclusive after 1640, when all other Western traders were expelled from Japan. This relationship lasted unbroken until Japan opened to the West in the 1850s, and it provided the shogunate with Western goods and information on the outside world during a period when the *sakoku* policy, the closure of the country, was rigidly enforced.[1]

Copper, gold and camphor were the main commodities bought by the Dutch East India Company in Japan, whereas silk, porcelain and lacquer were much less important. Nevertheless, these luxury goods are now regarded as among the most significant examples of the interaction in material culture between Japan and the West. Japanese export porcelain, in particular, is still abundantly available in Western collections and has been studied intensively.[2] Thanks to the documentation in VOC records, we have obtained a fairly good survey of shipments, prices and Dutch preferences for particular types of Arita wares.[3] Study of the pieces themselves has resulted in stylistic groupings, knowledge of the intermingling of motifs and decorative patterns and an insight into developments over time. Archaeological excavations in Arita have revealed information on potting and firing techniques and on the identification of kilns that made specific wares, including export porcelain.[4]

Less is known, however, about the reception of Japanese porcelain in the Netherlands and elsewhere in Europe. Was it regarded as more exclusive than Chinese porcelain, and was it more expensive?[5] How well did local appraisers distinguish between Japanese and Chinese porcelains, and can we trust their descriptions in contemporary inventories? Were all types of Japanese export porcelain in demand in the West, or were there regional differences in apprecia-tion, for instance between Germany and France? How was porcelain distributed in Holland and abroad after it reached Amsterdam? How did Japanese porcelain fare against Chinese competition after c. 1680? Some of these questions can be partially answered by looking at the influence of Japanese export wares on European ceramics between c. 1660 and 1800. Stylistic developments in various Western factories can indicate how fashionable and profitable a Japanese style of decoration may have been for different producers. Here I offer a short survey of the history of the trade in Japanese export porcelain, followed by a discussion on the influence these wares had in Europe.

TRADE IN CHINESE PORCELAIN

Until the mid-1640s, the Dutch East India Company bought Chinese porcelain from Chinese merchants who shipped it at their own risk either to Batavia (modern Jakarta in Indonesia) or to the Company's stronghold on Taiwan, which had been established in 1624.[6] The Taiwan depot was conveniently close to the Chinese mainland and allowed a continuous flow of Chinese goods, including late Ming porcelain, into Dutch storerooms. Stylistically, two groups can be distinguished within these Chinese export porcelains. The first is the so-called *kraak* porcelain, developed by the Chinese for maritime trade during the second half of the sixteenth century.[7] Chinese merchants distributed *kraak* porcelain to markets all over Southeast Asia and Japan, and Muslim traders sold it in India, on the east coast of Africa and in the Middle East. The Portuguese, who held a monopoly on trade between Asia and Europe in the sixteenth century, also bought *kraak* for their trade settlements in Goa, Malacca and Japan, as well as for the Portuguese home market. When Dutch and English merchants arrived in Asia around 1600, they complied with the existing conventions and also participated in this porcelain trade.

The Dutch East India Company brought such large amounts of *kraak* porcelain to the Netherlands that within a few decades it was found in the households of many Dutch burghers. In fact, the Dutch reduced Chinese porcelains from luxury goods, fit for the nobility and wealthy only, to popular exotic commodities, fit for everyday use and decoration. *Kraak*—named after the Portuguese carracks that shipped it—was mass-produced in Jingdezhen in a modular, almost industrial way. It is thinly potted, with edges that often have a retracting glaze. Kiln grit adheres to the footring or bottom. The decorations in underglaze cobalt blue are standardized and show river scenes with waterfowl, flowers and rocks, deer, insects and occasionally a human figure or a mythological animal. These central scenes are confined within complicated formal patterns; the rim usually has a border of large and small alternating panels filled with auspicious symbols. Because of its wide distribution and popularity, *kraak* became a model and a source of inspiration for later Japanese and European wares.

In the last decades of the Ming dynasty the imperial court stopped placing orders for porcelain, which created serious problems for the kilns in Jingdezhen. New markets had to be found, and from about 1620 several new types of export ware were introduced. For export to Japan, new types of underglaze blue *(ko-sometsuke)* and enamelled wares *(ko-akae)* were developed, the shapes and decorations of which were often based on Japanese models or demands.[8] For export to Europe, the Chinese produced so-called transitional-style porcelains—wares with a rather thick, smooth body, an impeccable glaze and figural designs based on Chinese literary sources.[9] Some of these transitional wares were shaped after Western models, such as beer mugs, mustard pots and salt-cellars. Most of the wares sent to Europe were decorated in underglaze blue; polychrome enamelled wares also were sent to Europe, but in much smaller quantities than might be expected. Transitional-style porcelain was produced for the Chinese market as well, and it is not always easy to distinguish between domestic and export wares. Transitional porcelain of typical Chinese shape and decoration is often encountered in old Western collections. These modern and fashionable transitional porcelains—usually closed shapes such as ewers, pots and jars—existed alongside the traditional *kraak* dishes and bowls.[10] Because of their innovative features they were a great success in Holland and very profitable for the Company. However, this situation did not last long. The Ming dynasty fell in 1644, and chaos reigned. Soon the porcelain industry in Jingdezhen could not cope with foreign orders because roads and waterways were blocked and deliveries became irregular. In the following decades, only small consignments of Chinese porcelain were occasionally exported by private merchants.

THE IMPACT ON ARITA AND DELFT

The shortage of Chinese porcelain at the end of the 1640s had an immediate impact in Japan and in Holland. Both markets reacted in a similar way: namely, by stimulating the production of already existing domestic ceramic industries.

In Japan, the kilns in Arita developed rapidly and competed fiercely to fill the gap in the market by producing a larger, much more varied output of high-quality Shoki-Imari wares. Polychrome enamel wares, influenced partly by Chinese *ko-sometsuke* and Swatow wares and partly by Kyoto enamelling techniques, were produced in a wide range of highly innovative shapes and designs. Underglaze blue wares also showed a similar degree of innovation and complexity. Between c. 1640 and 1660, the kilns in Arita were enlarged and reorganized; some shifted from stoneware production to porcelain, and many new ones were built.[11] It is not clear yet how this process of innovation was financed, but it may be assumed that, as in China, different groups of Japanese merchants took part, shared risks and probably guaranteed sales.

In Holland, the town of Delft became the centre of ceramic activity, taking over that position from Haarlem. Potters had long practised in Delft, their relatively small factories making tiles and utility earthenware. Polychrome-decorated wares were not unusual in Delft but were produced in a limited palette, based on the sixteenth-century traditions of Antwerp maiolica from the southern Netherlands. Blue decorations were more popular, quicker to produce and cheaper. The Delft industry got a boost when the shortage of Chinese porcelain became apparent to the Dutch public in the late 1640s. Demand for close imitations, even if made of earthenware, grew to such an extent that, as in Japan, potteries expanded and new techniques, new shapes and new decorations were introduced. Many new factories were founded, producing mainly blue and white wares decorated in Chinese *kraak* and transitional styles or various pastiches of the two.[12]

THE JAPANESE PORCELAIN TRADE OF THE DUTCH EAST INDIA COMPANY

In Japan, the Dutch East India Company, which since 1641 had been located on the fan-shaped artificial island of Deshima in Nagasaki Bay, was aware of the intensified activities in nearby Arita. Company employees privately bought Japanese porcelains (how interesting it would be to know what they preferred!) and made profits reselling them in Batavia and the Netherlands. When the Batavia government became aware of this trade, an order was placed, as an experiment, for a small assortment of apothecary pots made of Japanese porcelain but in Western shapes. In 1652, a shipment of 1,265 pieces was delivered to Taiwan. The following year, 2,200 flasks and albarelli (medicine jars) destined for the central apothecary in Batavia were shipped from Japan by the Company.[13] When these and subsequent orders proved to be satisfactory, the Amsterdam directors decided to join in the Japanese porcelain trade. In 1656 they ordered from Japan "a batch of porcelain because it was found that much was being brought by many private persons."[14] In answer, a crate with samples of Japanese porcelain that Company officials thought would probably sell well in Holland was sent from Deshima in 1657, arriving in Holland in summer 1658. Reacting quickly, the directors gave orders to buy an assortment of Japanese porcelain for Holland and indicated their preferences for certain types. Unfortunately, this order and its specifications got lost on its way to Deshima. Zacharias Wagenaer was VOC director in Japan in 1659. Although he knew he was supposed to send more porcelains back to Holland, he did not know what exactly was wanted, so he relied on the samples sent earlier. Furthermore, on his own initiative he ordered some pieces to be made in Arita after European models, such as ewers, mustard pots and wine jugs, which were decorated with small tendrils in silver on a monochrome underglaze blue ground. These "Wagenaer" pieces and a large assortment of over five thousand mostly polychrome wares were sent to Holland in 1659.[15] In the same year, much more Japanese porcelain was sent to Taiwan, Batavia, Surat, Bengal and Mocha, illustrating that the inter-Asian porcelain trade of the Dutch East India Company was equally important as the European trade, if not more so.[16] Shipments to Holland and several Asian markets continued in 1660 and thereafter on an even larger scale, yielding handsome profits to the Company.

JAPANESE ENAMELLED WARES

The sale of the 1657 samples was a great success in Holland and so were the following shipments. The success was undoubtedly owing to the presence of so many novel shapes unknown to the Dutch public, such as small human and animal figures, covered boxes, faceted cups and square and lozenge-shaped dishes.[17] Above all, the buyers were attracted to the bright enamels. Although the Chinese had produced some enamelled transitional porcelain for the Dutch at the end of the Ming dynasty, the public in the West largely associated Chinese porcelain with underglaze blue wares and was not aware of the polychrome types. The Japanese pieces, coloured with dark red, yellow, green, brown, even gold and silver, must have come as a great surprise to those who were sensitive to new and exotic things. A fashion was created, and right from the beginning enamelled wares formed a substantial part of all VOC porcelain shipments from Japan.

Of course, there were also customers in Batavia and Holland who were more old-fashioned and preferred the traditional underglaze blue porcelains that they were used to. And there were others who demanded tableware in Western forms, a category that had been highly successful in Chinese transitional porcelain. Japanese potters, realizing the importance of the Dutch to their expanding industry, were eager to please all of these groups. Thus in the decades after 1660 the Arita kilns responded to Dutch demand for porcelains in the following three categories: enamelled wares, largely decorated in Japanese style; underglaze blue wares in an imitation of Chinese *kraak* and transitional porcelain; and *commande* porcelain copying Western shapes such as spittoons, mugs and ewers. Naturally, these categories overlapped. For instance, there were dishes with *kraak* patterns done in overglaze enamels, which were destined not for the Netherlands but for the inter-Asian porcelain trade of the Dutch East India Company. And there were new forms like the *kendi,* modelled on a traditional South Asian water vessel, which was ordered for markets in Southeast Asia and was not part of the shipments to Holland.[18]

Within the underglaze blue wares made specifically for the Dutch East India Company, there was a gradual evolution from an interesting mixture of Chinese and Japanese decorative styles to a style in which Japanese patterns and motifs predominated. European motifs are almost completely absent, apart from the albarelli and flasks decorated with Latin initials[19] and the well-known dishes with the VOC monogram. This absence is odd because, if a Japanese potter could make a jug after a Western model, the decorator could have copied a Western scene. But apparently such *commande* designs were not produced until the eighteenth century. In any case, until c. 1680, most objects shaped after European models were painted in underglaze blue, as were the Japanese copies of Chinese *kraak* and transitional designs. Only occasionally do we see an enamelled, Western-shaped mug, ewer or ink set, but such exceptions may have been ordered for Batavia.

EXPORT WARES AND DOMESTIC WARES

Archaeological evidence has shown that several kilns in the Arita area produced porcelain for the Dutch East India Company. For instance, shards of underglaze blue albarelli, mugs, ewers and VOC dishes have been found at the kiln sites of Chokichidani, Shimoshirakawa, Tani, Hiekoba and Sarukawa. Remains of dishes, bowls and bottles decorated in *kraak* or transitional style were excavated at the kiln sites mentioned above, at Hokaoyama, Kakiemon and Nakashirakawa and at Aka-e-machi, the enamellers' quarter.[20] In addition to export wares, these and other kilns also produced a wide assortment of wares painted in underglaze blue with Japanese motifs and intended primarily for the domestic market. These domestic wares appealed to the Dutch as well and were appreciated as new and exotic, though it is not easy to distinguish them on the Deshima shipping lists. But certainly sake kettles, angular or leaf-shaped dishes, incense burners, tiered boxes *(jubako),* saucers with "Japanese letters" and fan-shaped dishes were included in export shipments around 1660. Furthermore, examples of these early Japanese-style blue and white pieces are still present in old European collections, such as those of Burghley House[21] or the former collection of Augustus the Strong in Dresden.[22] A lobed dish of this type is depicted in a still life by the Dutch painter Simon Luttichuys (1610–1661).[23] Another proof that these typical domestic-style pieces circulated in Europe in the second half of the seventeenth century is provided by a recent acquisition in the collection of the Groningen Museum in the Netherlands. This piece is a very rare, unmarked Dutch Delft dish of c. 1660–80, painted blue with a bold border design of connected leaves in which a vein pattern has been reserved in a lighter blue.[24] The decoration is unlike traditional Delft painting but closely resembles the *sumi hajiki* technique (painting with ink) that was popular on domestic Arita wares of the 1660s.[25] Even more telling is the central design, showing two squares at an angle on top of each other, the upper one depicting a Chinese transitional design of figures in a landscape. This design of squares is a close copy of a pattern used on a specific type of underglaze blue Japanese dish; the pattern represents *shikishi,* paper squares used for painting or calligraphy.[26]

EARLY ENAMELLED WARES

Oliver Impey coined the term "Early Enamelled Wares" to describe the polychrome export porcelains produced between the late 1650s and c. 1670.[27] They are characterized by bright, rather opaque enamels such as green, a dark yellow, aubergine and overglaze blue, often combined with a dull brick red. Although some scholars have stated that the overglaze blue was a Japanese invention, probably based on enamelled Kyoto earthenware,[28] I would like to suggest the possibility of direct influence from Chinese Swatow wares, on which a turquoise blue was often applied. Swatow, produced in southern China in the Pinghe area of Fujian province, was frequently imported into Japan, appreciated widely and thus could well have been a source of inspiration.[29] Early Enamelled Wares also included pieces partly or completely painted with silver or gold, though the production of silver-decorated wares was relatively short-lived because of silver's tendency to tarnish and turn black. How enamelling for the different kilns in Arita was organized is not clear, but it was obviously done by specialized workshops and not in the factories that made the actual pieces because no wasters of enamelled wares are found at the kiln sites. An excavation at the site of the former post office in Arita yielded part of what is regarded as the Aka-e-machi, an enamellers' quarter, and probably more such places existed.

Of course, enamelling itself continued the Arita traditions of the pre-1660 Shoki-Imari wares, but on the export wares the coloured decorations in purely Japanese style of flowers, plants, birds and an occasional landscape are less varied and may reflect a simplification of the process, owing to the stress of coping with the huge orders from the Company. As mentioned above, another category of early enamels imitated Chinese *kraak* wares. Still another category, the more exuberant and darker so-called Ko-Kutani wares, now proven to be made in Arita, was likely produced for the inter-Asian trade and exported by the Dutch or the Chinese.

In discussing the porcelain trade in general, it is useful to ask who exactly exported what. The Japanese themselves were confined within their borders and were not permitted to engage in maritime trade. The Dutch East India Company transported huge quantities of goods from Japan, and fortunately we have the documentation on orders and shipments. Private trade was also allowed, but these cargoes were not documented. Impey has evaluated the numbers of exported porcelains recorded in the Nagasaki customs ledgers (extant only for 1709 to 1711), and the differences between what the Dutch stated they bought and what the Japanese officials said they sold to the Dutch are striking. In 1710, for instance, the VOC recorded the purchase of 10,940 pieces, whereas the customs ledgers report a sale of 158,578 pieces![30] We can only assume that the difference reflected the level of private trade; in the 1660s there may have been a similar discrepancy between VOC records and the actual quantity of Dutch exports. Needless to say, privately bought Japanese porcelain must therefore have been available in Batavia.

Further complicating matters is the fact that the Chinese, who had a much larger trade settlement in Nagasaki than the Dutch, also bought Japanese porcelain and resold it to Western traders in Amoy, Taiwan, Canton and probably even in Batavia. Evidence for this trade is found in the bills of lading of English ships returning from Canton to London in the early eighteenth century that frequently mention Japanese wares, as do the London auction catalogues. Furthermore, British East India Company documents give instructions to buy Japanese wares from the Chinese in Amoy and Canton.[31] This circumvention of the Dutch monopoly on trade with Japan might partly explain the wide distribution of all kinds of pre-1700 Japanese porcelain in England. More controversial is the question of whether Kakiemon was part of this Chinese trade (which I think most likely) and if Kakiemon was made to Chinese taste (which I think unlikely because of the absence of Chinese motifs).[32]

KAKIEMON

Classic polychrome Kakiemon gradually emerged from Early Enamelled Ware in the 1670s.[33] It is characterized by a more refined and often asymmetrical decoration in softer-coloured enamels on an impeccable glaze, very carefully painted, giving an almost miniaturist effect. Use of very well-levigated clay of outstanding quality from a particular area in the Izumiyama pit resulted in the highly praised *nigoshide* body, which produced a milk-white ground for the enamelling. This type of body was never used for large pieces, figures or for underglaze blue Kakiemon. Kakiemon decoration includes an array of motifs, such as a bound bamboo hedge, a flying or perched bird with a long tail (referred to as a "phoenix" in Western sources), a tiger near a bamboo grove, a dragon or *shishi,* butterflies, quails, flowering plants and blossoming prunus (plum) trees. Human figures, usually women or children, occur occasionally. A wide variety of decorative geometric patterns are used as borders. Marks do not appear on enamelled pieces but are commonly found on underglaze blue Kakiemon, which also shows a wider array of motifs, including landscapes and river scenes. A sub-group combines an underglaze blue design with overglaze enamels. The enamelled three-dimensional figures of elephants, horses and *bijin* (beautiful women) rank among the most luxurious and exotic items made for export. Strangely, no underglaze blue examples of the figures are known.

The Kakiemon kiln was most likely founded in the Nangawara area in the 1670s, according to Impey,[34] and flourished between c. 1680 and the late 1720s, when the workshops were temporarily closed down, only to resume production some time afterward. Today, Sakaida Kakiemon XIV, a direct descendant and a living national treasure, continues the tradition.

Before the Kakiemon kiln in Nangawara was founded, it seems that an enamellers' workshop was already active, though it is difficult to distinguish its products from other early enamelled wares. Probably, the opportunity to make *nigoshide* wares in the new *noborigama* kiln triggered the creation of a unique Kakiemon style. In any case, the kiln and the enamelling workshop (wherever it may have been situated) worked as a unit, though it is unknown if it was an exclusive cooperation or if other kiln owners could have had their wares painted there, too.

It is widely assumed that during this period of fame, when the kiln's output was large, much, if not all, Kakiemon porcelain was produced for export. According to Japanese specialists it was not appreciated and sold on the domestic market; only rarely are shards found in city excavations in Japan. Nevertheless, it seems strange that a factory that is said to have produced porcelain almost exclusively for export made so few pieces with Western designs and/or shapes; the Japanese "feel" of their products is almost tangible. More research is therefore needed to determine if Japanese consumers, always keen to absorb enamelled wares of good quality, did not have an influence after all.[35]

IMARI

Imari porcelain was another offspring of Early Enamelled Ware. This group is widely divergent and includes pieces painted in underglaze blue with an overglaze decoration of iron-red and gold, sometimes with added black or green; other pieces have just enamelled decoration. It is a typical export product with many different Western shapes and a huge variety of motifs and patterns, sometimes copied from Western models. The general appearance of Imari is less light and refined than Kakiemon, but their compact compositions and dense patterns appealed to the Dutch and other Europeans in the Baroque period. The style matured in the 1670s, as did Kakiemon, and in the following years it became highly popular and was the main output of many kilns in Arita. Although export waned after c. 1740, Imari never went out of fashion and is still produced in several factories in Arita.[36] As the Macdonald Collection does not focus on Imari, a more detailed discussion is not needed here and can be found elsewhere.

DECLINE

In China, the Kangxi emperor (r. 1662–1722) gradually overcame the last gasps of Ming resistance in the early 1680s, and within a few years the porcelain factories in Jingdezhen started export production again. Maritime trade flourished and Chinese traders set out to re-conquer their lost markets in Asia. Soon Chinese junks appeared in Batavia to sell porcelain and to take orders from the Dutch.[37] Prices were low, the quality and variety of the Chinese wares were good, and Japanese potters, producing on a smaller scale, simply could not compete. In 1683 the VOC, wary of high prices, order complications and incomplete deliveries in Japan, decided to cease buying Japanese porcelain for Holland, though it continued to order Japanese porcelain for the Southeast Asian trade. As stated above, private Dutch East India Company employees in Deshima, as well as Chinese traders, continued to export Arita wares, and therefore much of the Kakiemon and Imari porcelain in the West was not handled by the Company, but bought and distributed by other parties.

DUTCH DELFTWARES

In the second quarter of the seventeenth century, imported Chinese porcelain began to influence potting and firing techniques in Holland.[38] Traditional maiolica was rather sturdy and economical to produce; only the front of a dish was covered with a white-firing tin glaze, whereas the back had a transparent lead glaze. Competition with porcelain forced the potters to make a thinner body, to cover it on both sides with tin glaze and to use stoneware cylinders to prevent ash and dirt from spoiling the surfaces of the pieces during firing. Metal pins stuck through the sides of the cylinders provided a support for the flat wares stacked inside, leaving an imprint in the glaze of the back. This new product became known as faience, or, as the potters proudly promoted it, "Delft porcelain." Outside Holland too, potters were quick to advertise their faience as an alternative for porcelain; for instance, an English potter in Southwark who in 1638 already declared that he had invented "white earthenware pots glazed both within and without which show as fair as Chinese dishes."[39] Of course, this faience was just fine earthenware, the body coloured yellowish or reddish after a first biscuit firing at about 900 degrees Celsius. Then the piece was covered with a tin glaze, painted with blue or fire-resistant enamels on top of the glaze and fired a second time in the *grand feu* (high-temperature firing). Because there was plenty of real porcelain around, decorations on early faience were not usually done in the Chinese style; on the contrary, the selling point was the Western-style decoration, which was not available in porcelain.

All this changed at the end of the 1640s when Chinese porcelain became scarce and the Dutch East India Company could no longer meet the continuing public demand for it. Delftware, which resembled porcelain (particularly from a distance) but was much cheaper, was ideal as a replacement, as long as it had Chinese-style decoration. The few factories in Delft that dared adapt their production to make close imitations of *kraak* and transitional porcelain met with immediate success. In a very short time they expanded their efforts and were joined by other potters as Delft quickly became a centre of faience production. Whereas there were only three or four factories in Delft in 1647, there were over twenty in 1661 and more than thirty by the end of the century. The Delft potters even managed to take over part of the former re-export trade in Chinese porcelain, selling their products to France, Germany, England and Scandinavia, notwithstanding fierce competition from earthenware factories in those countries that also speedily applied Chinese motifs on their products.

POLYCHROME DELFT

Initially, Chinese-style Delftware was painted in blue to conform to the original models, though Delft painters quickly invented a style of their own, adapting Chinese motifs and rendering them in new, inventive combinations that emphasized their Oriental exoticism. The imports of Japanese polychrome porcelain that began in the early 1660s made many Dutch consumers aware for the first time of Oriental porcelain that was not blue and white. This imported polychrome porcelain was relatively scarce and expensive; thus there was a ready market for imitations. From about 1670 one sees the development of coloured Delftware, with yellow, purple, green, brown and some shades of red in the *grand feu*. The cessation of Japanese porcelain imports by the Dutch East India Company in 1683 provided an incentive for the further development of polychrome Delft, which was also stimulated by the imports of enamelled Chinese porcelain like *famille verte* at the end of the seventeenth century.

Going beyond copying the specific decorations, Delft potters wished to imitate the colour schemes of Kakiemon and Imari wares; but in this the potters encountered problems. The gold and brick red that were typical of Imari, and the softer enamel colours that were typical of Kakiemon, could not be used because they burned away in the heat of the *grand feu.* After experimenting with different techniques, Dutch potters eventually learned to use the muffle kiln around or shortly before 1700. Pieces already glazed and fired could be decorated with enamels and fired for a third time in the muffle kiln at a lower temperature of approximately 600 degrees Celsius. This lower-temperature firing came to be known as the *petit feu.* The new type of polychrome ware was relatively costly because of the risky three-stage firing process and the use of expensive enamels. It had a limited distribution and only a few factories, like De Grieksche A, De Dobbelde Schenkkan and De Drie Vergulde Astonnekens specialized in the *petit feu.* Those pieces that copy Japanese Imari in blue, gold, red and some green or black are traditionally called the Delft Imari group. Interestingly, polychrome copies of Kakiemon designs never were regarded as a category on their own, but it is clear that the stylistic distinction between Imari and Kakiemon was made. The Delft painters tried to capture the lightness and elegance of Kakiemon, using characteristic elements such as bamboo hedges, the bamboo grove, the flowering prunus, the "phoenix" and the strolling tiger. Sometimes the Delft decorators made close copies of Kakiemon wares, but more often they isolated different Kakiemon elements and then combined them in new compositions that appealed to the exotic tastes of the day.

When Delft painters copied Kakiemon designs, they must have followed models. And as they used a wide variety of different Kakiemon elements, the originals must have been fairly common in the Netherlands. However, we still have no firm information about the distribution and value of Kakiemon in the Netherlands during this period. The name Kakiemon does not appear in the West before the end of the nineteenth century; in contemporary documents it is not distinguished from the other polychrome Arita porcelains. In eighteenth-century auction catalogues, newspapers or inventories only rarely is there a clear indication that the object described is a Kakiemon piece. For instance, an advertisement in the *Amsterdamse Courant* of August 26, 1751, mentions a sale of porcelain, including dishes of various sizes with the "famous age-old Japanese man in the well," octagonal with brown rims—a clear reference to the "Hob in the Well" (Shiba Onko) design. Another advertisement for a porcelain auction in the same newspaper of November 5, 1750, mentions "ribbed dishes and saucers with brown rims and the leaping tiger and reed bushes," which could describe either blue and white or enamelled Kakiemon.[40]

DELFT-DECORATED IMPORTED PORCELAINS

An interesting side effect of the introduction of the muffle kiln was the emergence around 1700 of a new category of porcelains known as Amsterdams Bont that were imported as blanks from Asia and decorated with polychrome enamels in the Netherlands.[41] Because muffle kilns were fired at a low temperature, they could be used in smaller workshops away from the porcelain factories. Thus dishes, ewers, bowls, bottles and other objects of Chinese or, less commonly, Japanese, porcelain imported into the Netherlands could be painted in enamels with chinoiserie or Kakiemon designs and fired economically in small batches. Originally, these Asian porcelains were either plain white, without decorations, or painted sparingly in underglaze blue. By embellishing them with enamels, the decorators in Holland thus made them more attractive and saleable. The Kakiemon designs on these wares were often carefully painted and imitate their Japanese models quite closely. This practice clearly indicates that Kakiemon was valued as something special and distinct from other Chinese and Japanese enamelled porcelain.

In view of the technical skill and experience needed for polychrome enamelling, it can be assumed that the vast majority of this work was done in Delft; but some of it may have been done elsewhere, possibly in tile factories that engaged independent painters working at home to apply the decoration. It is difficult to date this Dutch-decorated Asian porcelain as we have no documentation on the production process; nor is there much evidence of stylistic progress. The more carefully painted, detailed pieces may date to the early eighteenth century, whereas the more common ones with standardized patterns, often painted over an original underglaze blue decoration, may be later. In any case, the added value of these wares must have diminished after the early 1730s when the Dutch East India Company began importing Chinese porcelain in great quantity and variety from Canton, including polychrome wares such as Chinese Imari and *famille rose.* The exceptions may have been the pieces decorated with Kakiemon designs, because, strangely, Kakiemon was very rarely copied by the Chinese, and demand for this style continued in Holland.

VOC imports from China caused a decline in the Delft production in general, especially of those pieces that were decorated in an Oriental style. The only factories to survive were those that made special shapes not available in Chinese porcelain or that focused on Western designs. Oriental decorations, including those in Kakiemon style, returned briefly in the last quarter of the eighteenth century on Dutch porcelain made in Loosdrecht and Amstel. However, such pieces do not reflect a renewed interest in exotic designs and were most likely made as replacements or additions to existing sets.

EUROPEAN PORCELAIN IMITATIONS

As mentioned above, we have little information about how Kakiemon was distributed in Europe. During its heyday, Kakiemon was sold in Deshima to private Dutch traders or via the Chinese to English and probably French merchants. After it reached Europe it was auctioned or sold to specialized shops that dealt in Oriental goods. Interested buyers would have bought assortments or individual pieces for their own use, for other parties or for wholesale re-export to other countries. It is clear that there must have been a wide interest in these wares, given the still extant pieces in old European collections and the imitations made in the eighteenth century in European porcelain factories. It seems, however, that such imitations were not made before the end of the 1720s, when the production of good-quality Kakiemon came to an end.[42]

GERMANY

Meissen, near Dresden, was the first factory in the West to produce hard-paste porcelain after the formula for its manufacture was discovered by Böttger and von Tschirnhaus in 1708.[43] The driving force behind the factory was Augustus the Strong (1670–1733), Elector of Saxony and King of Poland, who became a passionate collector of Asian porcelain, amassing huge quantities of Chinese and Japanese wares. Meissen wares from the first years of production show a variety of Chinese and chinoiserie designs, but very few designs inspired by Japanese models. This changed in the late 1720s, when Meissen began producing beautiful porcelains in the Kakiemon style, often closely copying the shapes and decoration of Japanese originals.[44] Some examples are so well made that even specialists sometimes have difficulty distinguishing the original (if it is not marked) from the copy. Other varieties have Kakiemon-style decoration in panels on a monochrome ground or use the Kakiemon pictorial elements in a free way. It is obvious that the Kakiemon style in particular was favoured, because Meissen porcelain imitating Imari is much rarer.[45]

The fashion for Kakiemon-style porcelains at Meissen lasted until the early 1740s, when European subjects took over. The models for the Meissen Kakiemon wares were most likely provided by Augustus the Strong from his own collection. How he had acquired them is still a subject of research, but there are indications that he ordered his ambassadors in the Netherlands to buy whatever they considered interesting and rare. He also bought frequently from dealers, such as Elisabeth Bassetouche. In addition, Asian porcelain enamelled in Holland in the Kakiemon style may have been sold to him as the real thing. However, to complicate the matter, white Meissen porcelain was also enamelled in the Kakiemon palette in Holland! In connection to this practice, the Lemaire episode, as recounted by Mallet, is most interesting.[46] In 1728, the French dealer Rodolphe Lemaire bought undecorated Meissen porcelain and sent the pieces to Holland to be enamelled "in the taste of the colours of old Japan," intending them to serve as models for Meissen copies. In 1729 he and Graf von Hoym, minister to Augustus and director of the Meissen factory, started producing Meissen porcelain in the Kakiemon style but without the usual crossed swords factory mark. Lemaire suggested that he could sell these copies as genuine Japanese pieces, which indicates that Kakiemon was much sought after and that these "fakes" could yield high profits. Von Hoym fell into disgrace in 1731 and the enterprise came to a shameful end, but in the meantime much excellent Meissen porcelain in the Kakiemon style had been made and sold.

FRANCE

The intention to make porcelain of the quality of "old Japan" is also apparent in the patent for Chantilly in 1735. Japanese Kakiemon had become a mark of quality and status, and imitating it was a sure way to make profits. In France, the soft-paste factories of Chantilly, Saint-Cloud and Mennecy in particular reflect

the Kakiemon influence in their wares. The Chantilly factory was formally founded in 1735, but experimental work may have begun some ten years earlier, supported by Louis-Henri, the prince de Condé (1692–1740), who was exiled from the French court to his castle at Chantilly. He, like Augustus the Strong, was an avid porcelain collector; the inventory drawn up at his death lists over two thousand pieces.[47] As at Meissen, Kakiemon pieces from this collection were used as models for the decoration of Chantilly pieces. The creamy

Fig. 11
PLATE WITH TIGER AND BAMBOO DESIGN
Germany, Meissen factory, c. 1728–31
D: 23.2 cm

surface lent itself very well to a restrained application of bright enamels in the Kakiemon palette, sometimes aiming at a straight copy, more often producing pieces of Western shape decorated in the Kakiemon style or influenced by Meissen porcelain. The same can be said of the products of the Saint-Cloud factory (founded in 1677) and of Villeroy-Mennecy (1734), both of which have a creamy or ivory-toned surface on which the bright enamels of the Kakiemon palette could be most favourably applied. By the mid-eighteenth century the interest in Oriental styles was waning in France, and Kakiemon-style decorations on porcelain from the Vincennes factory (founded in 1738) and its successor, Sèvres (1756), are rare.

ENGLAND

In England things were different. It was around 1750 that the Chelsea factory (founded in 1743) started to make porcelain decorated in the Kakiemon style on a large scale, precisely at the time when interest on the continent for such patterns had ended. Before then, the Kakiemon style, and Japanese motifs in general, had not been particularly popular in England, though they sometimes appear on early Chelsea pieces and also on some Chinese pieces that were imported as blanks and decorated in England. The reason for Chelsea's move into Kakiemon is unknown, but I suspect the fact that the factory was under the protection of William Augustus, Duke of Cumberland, from 1750 to 1758 was partly responsible. The duke would have been aware of the high status that Meissen, Chantilly and Saint-Cloud wares had among the continental nobility, particularly the pieces decorated in the refined and elegant Kakiemon style. Because such porcelains were no longer made, he may have envisioned their replacement by Chelsea products. Models from Meissen were provided by Sir Charles Hanbury Williams, a former envoy in Dresden, through the secretary of the duke, Sir Everard Fawkener, and undoubtedly from others as well. Inspiration was probably also derived directly from Japanese originals.[48] In any case, it is noteworthy that from about 1750 to the temporary closure of the factory in 1756, there was a substantial output of very well-made Chelsea wares closely copying Kakiemon designs or decorated in the Kakiemon palette; after the duke's death in 1758, the Kakiemon style was not revived. Chelsea wares have a rather thick tin glaze, which is a perfect ground for the carefully painted enamelled designs. Particularly in favour was the quail pattern, which also had

Fig. 12
DISH WITH BIRD ON A FLOWERING BRANCH
Italy, Milan, c. 1750–80
D: 23 cm

been fashionable in Meissen, Delft and the French factories. In England the two foraging birds were misnamed partridges; they are also called partridges in references to the output of other factories, such as Bow and Worcester.

The Bow and Worchester factories seem to have continued imitating Japanese and Kakiemon designs even after Chelsea stopped. Bow in London (patents in 1744 and 1749), also named "New Canton," specialized in Chinese-style decoration, but pieces in the Kakiemon style were made as well, in particular during the period 1755–60. As at Chelsea, some pieces were undoubtedly directly copied from Japanese originals, whereas others may have been based on European models decorated in the Kakiemon style. The designs are well painted, though sometimes slightly less fluent and elegant than decoration on the Chelsea wares. How important the antiquarian status of "old Japan" still was in England is evident from an advertisement from 1758 for an auction of Bow porcelain: "Some part of this Porcelain is very little inferior to the fine old browne Edge Japan and wants no other Recommendation than its own Beauty and Service."[49]

Founded in 1751, Worcester produced huge amounts of domestic wares. Kakiemon-style decorations, often in simplified form, appear mainly on wares from the period 1765–70, even later than at Chelsea and Bow, and seem to have been less important than the more numerous Worcester Imari imitations, which are closer to the originals. The Kakiemon palette was often used in panels on a monochrome ground, probably inspired by Chinese Kangxi powder-blue wares;[50] pieces copying Kakiemon wares in shape and decoration are rare. Nevertheless, the prestige of Japan was valued here too, as is evident from a sale catalogue of 1769, where mention is made of a "fine old Japan fan pattern," "fine old rich mosaic japan pattern," "scrole japan pattern" and other descriptions.[51]

Chelsea and Bow were the main producers of high-quality English porcelain with Kakiemon patterns; Worcester, Plymouth and Derby were less important. All these factories may have had difficulties selling their wares on the continent because there the public had lost interest in Oriental, and more specifically Kakiemon, designs. Late Rococo styles, and soon the Neoclassical fashion, made these "old" patterns seem outmoded.

Nevertheless, the fascination for the quality, the elegance of the asymmetrical designs, the detailed painting and the soft glowing enamels of Kakiemon lingered on, especially among collectors in France. As Clare Le Corbeiller stated, "Japanese porcelain had become a connoisseur's taste, at least in France, where 'Porcelaines de première qualité coloriée'" were placed ahead of other porcelains in eighteenth-century sale catalogues. It was this porcelain that was described in the Randon de Boisset sale (1777), "of which the composition is entirely lost, that has always inspired the greatest sensation among connoisseurs, for the fine grain of its beautiful white paste, the alluring softness of its matte red, the velvety tone of its soft and lively colours of green and deep *bleu celeste*; such is the true recognized merit of this porcelain; also all the best cabinets have it and are composed of it."[52] Nothing could better have described the fascination Kakiemon had in Europe, then and now.

PART II

HIGHLIGHTS OF THE MACDONALD COLLECTION

JAPANESE PORCELAIN:
EARLY BLUE AND WHITE WARES

Fig. 13
DISH WITH JOCULAR BIRD
Japan, Arita, c. 1640–50
D: 21.5 cm

THE EARLIEST JAPANESE PORCELAINS (called Shoki-Imari or "early Imari") had plain white surfaces or white surfaces painted with cobalt-blue designs beneath a clear glaze. Blue and white porcelain had been a major component of China's porcelain industry since the fourteenth century.[1] Developed initially for markets in the Islamic world, blue and white porcelain became popular within China during the early fifteenth century and soon afterward became an important export to other markets in East and Southeast Asia as well.

Chinese blue and white porcelains were first shipped to Japan in significant quantities during the late sixteenth and early seventeenth centuries. There the porcelains were greatly esteemed by wealthy samurai and merchants as symbols of good taste and high status. After the Japanese discovered the formula for making porcelain in the 1610s, the early workshops concentrated on making blue and white wares because they were so much in demand and were relatively easy to produce.[2]

The initial Japanese blue and white porcelains were often pitted and warped, with dark, smudgy cobalt designs and underfired grey grounds. But within a decade or so, the quality of the domestic product improved considerably. Potters experimented with more difficult techniques and more complex designs and created pieces that expressed a more distinctly Japanese aesthetic. Although blue and white wares were overshadowed by enamel-decorated porcelains in the second half of the seventeenth century, they remained popular in the domestic Japanese market and were widely used throughout the eighteenth and nineteenth centuries.

Fig. 14
SMALL DISH WITH STYLIZED LANDSCAPE
Japan, Arita, c. 1620–30
D: 13.4 cm

Small food dishes made up a large proportion of the earliest Japanese blue and white porcelains. In the seventeenth and eighteenth centuries, formal Japanese meals often consisted of several different courses that were served to diners individually on small dishes such as these.[3] The dishes were typically produced in sets of five or ten, and tended to feature fairly simple, nature-inspired designs.[4] The small size of the dishes was partly a matter of their function and partly a matter of the available production technology. The earliest Japanese porcelains were fired without saggars (fireclay boxes) to protect them from scorching flames and flying ash inside the kiln. Because large objects faced a higher risk of being spoiled during the firing process, potters preferred to keep their wares small to minimize their losses. The bodies of the dishes were frequently somewhat grey as a result of insufficient firing temperatures and the presence of titanium in the clay.

Fig. 15
SMALL DISH WITH BUTTERFLY AND FLOWERS
Japan, Arita, c. 1620–40
D: 14.1 cm

Fig. 16
PAIR OF SMALL DISHES WITH GEESE AND REEDS
Japan, Arita, c. 1630–50
D: 15.5 cm

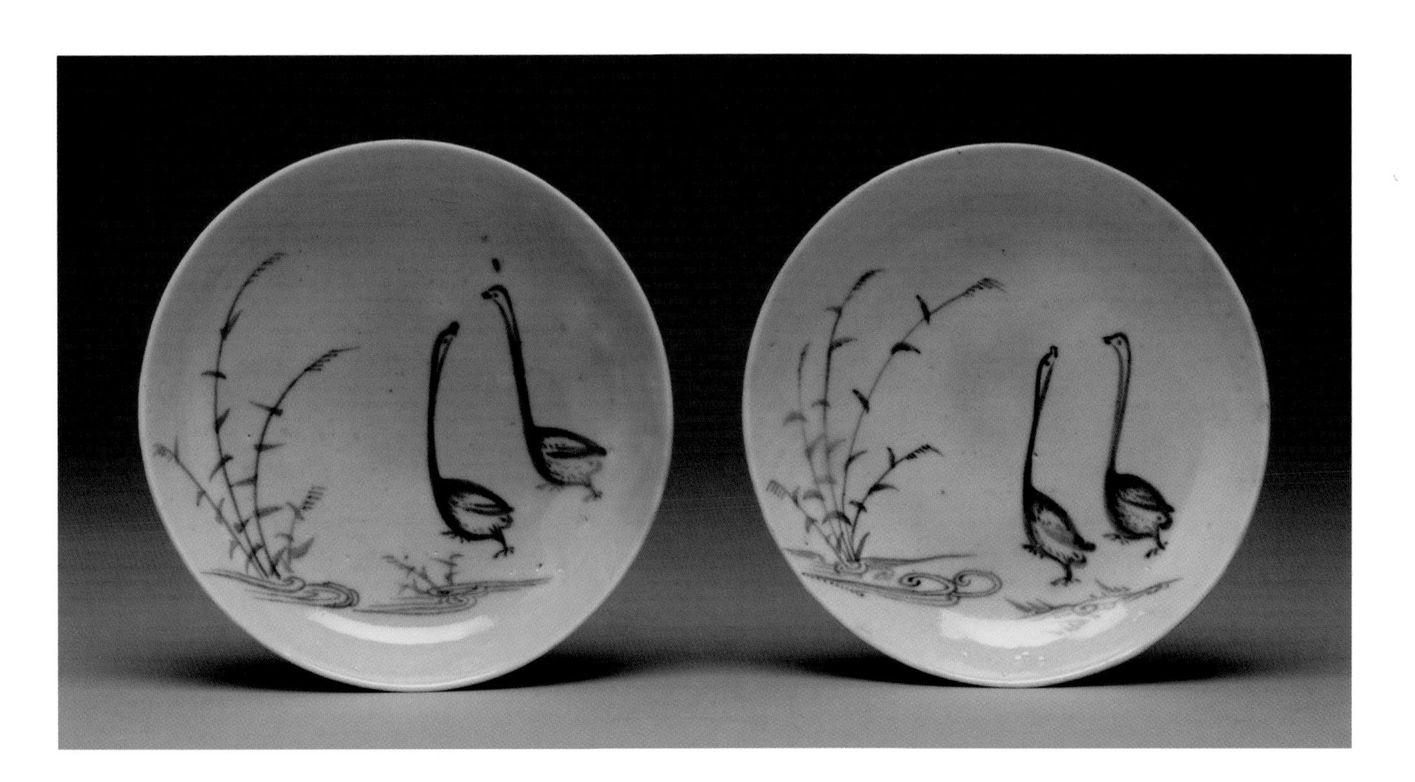

Fig. 17
DISH WITH CONCENTRIC CIRCLES AND BAMBOO
Japan, Arita, c. 1630–40
D: 22.1 cm

As Japanese potters gradually became more familiar with the materials and techniques used to produce porcelain, they began to pursue more ambitious forms and designs. This dish is decorated with an unusual design featuring several stalks of bamboo placed against a background of narrowly spaced concentric circles. The image strongly recalls the raked sand patterns and simple plantings of a Zen temple garden, yet also works very successfully as a semi-abstract, ornamental pattern. Bamboo was a traditional symbol of strength and resiliency in Japan and China. Because the brush strokes used to depict bamboo stalks and leaves were similar to those used in writing, bamboo painting was thought to be closely allied to calligraphy and was regarded as a telling measure of an artist's graphic skill.

Fig. 18
DISH WITH BLOWN-INK CRANE DESIGN
Japan, Arita, c. 1630–40
D: 20 cm

Fig. 19
SMALL DISH WITH STANDING EGRET
Japan, Arita, c. 1630–40
D: 15.3 cm

Fig. 20
BROWN-GLAZED DISH WITH STANDING EGRET
Japan, Arita, c. 1630–50
D: 22 cm

Early Japanese porcelain decorators frequently borrowed both designs and techniques from the textile industry. For example, the brown-glazed dish illustrated here was probably created using a wax resist technique similar to one used in silk dyeing.[5] To decorate the dish, the image of the bird was first painted with cobalt and covered with a clear glaze. The bird was then masked with wax and the plate was dipped in a thick iron-oxide glaze. When the plate was fired, the wax melted and the glazes set, creating the final appearance.[6]

Another decorative technique brought from textiles to porcelains was the use of stencils. The dish with the image of the two cranes was created by placing paper stencils on the surface of the dish and blowing a cobalt solution through a bamboo tube to produce a speckled ground around the shapes.[7] The stencils were then removed and the outlines of the cranes were drawn in using a brush.[8] The technique of blowing pigment through a tube *(fukizumi)* was also sometimes used by scroll and screen painters to depict snow and mist.

The third dish with the single egret motif may have been made using either a stencil or a resist technique. Here the decorator created a reserve image, contrasting the white clay of the dish body with a painted cobalt-blue ground.[9] Although the technique is simple, the final result is a highly evocative image of a bird standing in a pool of water with ripples spreading outward to the edge of the dish.

Fig. 21
PAIR OF VASES WITH POMEGRANATE DESIGN
Japan, Arita, c. 1650–60
H: 21 cm

Along with food dishes, many other functional and decorative forms were made in blue and white porcelain during the seventeenth century. The vases illustrated here were probably used for displaying seasonal flowers in a *tokonoma,* a decorative alcove that was an important feature of the reception rooms in many residences and in teahouses. The trumpet shapes of the vases were borrowed from Chinese ceramics and ultimately derive from ancient Chinese bronze forms. Because of their many seeds, pomegranates were popular symbols of fertility and prosperity in both Japanese and Chinese cultures.

The square jar may have been used for storing tea or medicine. Its form has precedents in China but is also similar to the square bottles that were used for storage on European ships.[10] Like several of the previous dishes, it is decorated with images of egrets. Egrets were a common sight along the Shirakawa River near Arita and were frequently celebrated as symbols of elegance in both Japanese and Chinese poetry and painting.

Fig. 22
SQUARE JAR
Japan, Arita, c. 1670
H: 11.5 cm

Fig. 23
SCALLOPED DISH WITH TIGER AND BAMBOO
Japan, Arita, c. 1650
D: 21.2 cm

One way Japanese potters met the rapidly rising demand for porcelain in the second half of the seventeenth century was by using moulds to speed up the production process.[11] The scalloped dish illustrated here represents one of the most common moulded shapes; examples exist that are painted with a wide variety of different subjects and decorative styles.[12] A nearly identical version of this dish, with its design of a tiger stalking through a bamboo grove, exists in the collection of the Kyushu Ceramic Museum in Japan and must have been produced by the same workshop.[13] The tiger and bamboo image is similar to those seen in some schools of Chinese and Japanese painting from the sixteenth and seventeenth centuries.[14]

The other two dishes are slightly later. The dish with the chrysanthemum design has a moulded border decorated with highly stylized images of flowers and leaves; the border of the dish with the egret design is decorated with an auspicious fungus design.[15] The range of tonal variation in the cobalt-blue paintings on these dishes demonstrates how advanced Japanese blue and white porcelain had become by the third quarter of the seventeenth century. The backs of all the dishes are inscribed with the character *fuku* ("good fortune"), a mark copied by the Japanese potters from Chinese porcelains of the late Ming period. (See p. 193 for a detail of the mark on fig. 23.)

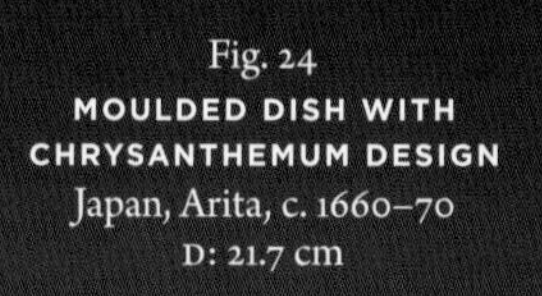

Fig. 24
MOULDED DISH WITH CHRYSANTHEMUM DESIGN
Japan, Arita, c. 1660–70
D: 21.7 cm

Fig. 25
MOULDED DISH WITH EGRET DESIGN
Japan, Arita, c. 1660–70
D: 21 cm

Fig. 26
SMALL DISH WITH ROUNDEL PATTERN
Japan, Arita, c. 1640
D: 15.1 cm

Fig. 27
DISH WITH SQUARE PLUM BLOSSOM PAINTING
Japan, Arita, c. 1660–70
D: 20.7 cm

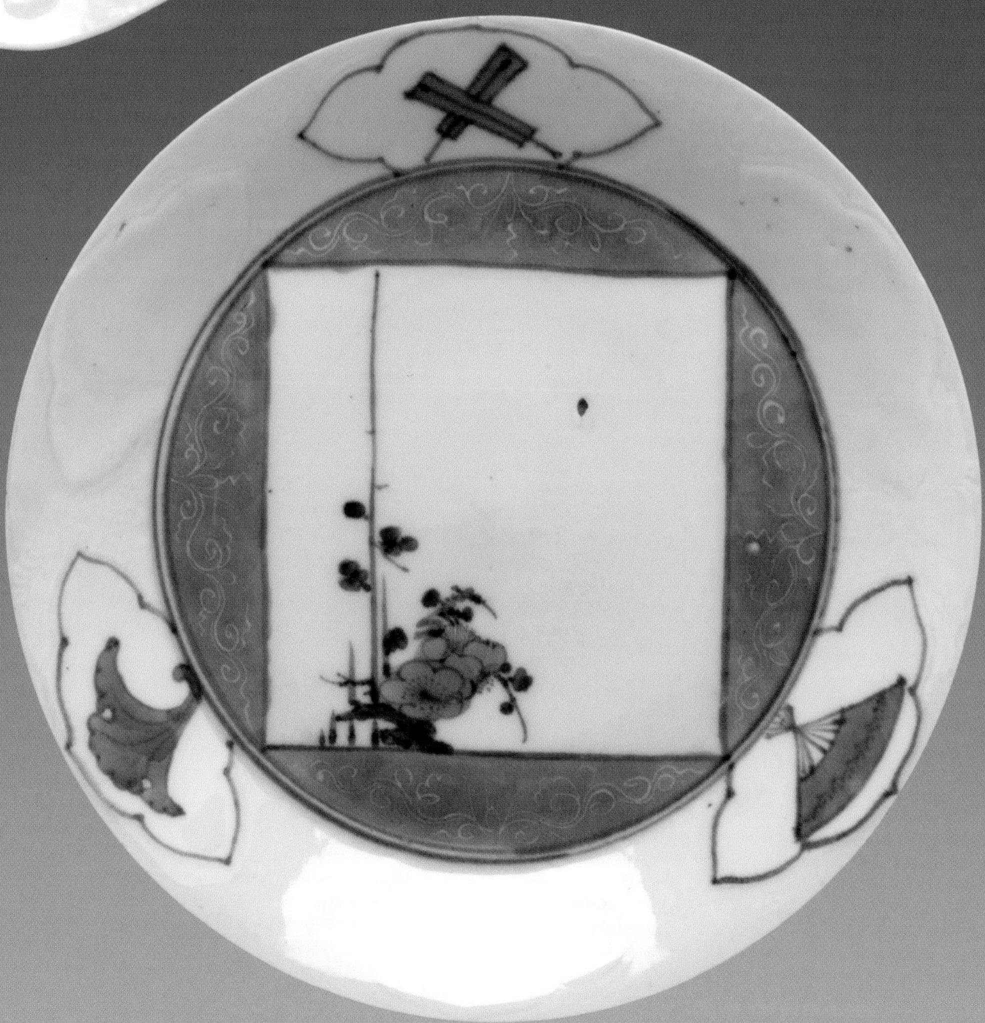

Japanese porcelain decorators drew on a wide range of both Chinese and Japanese sources for their designs. Some of the designs were representational and symbolic; other designs were more abstract and lyrical. The double peach design illustrated here is an example of the representational and symbolic category. In traditional Chinese and Japanese iconography, peaches were symbols of longevity, and images of multiple peaches were often used to express wishes for a long life.[16] The designs on the other two dishes belong to the more abstract and lyrical category. Roundels that had no meaning but were used to create interesting decorative patterns were a common motif on seventeenth-century Japanese porcelains and may have been inspired by contemporary textile and lacquer designs.[17] The square design of the plum blossom painting was inspired by *shikishi,* paper squares used for improvisational paintings and poems that were often created during the tea ceremony.[18] Numerous similar dishes reflect the popularity of this decorative motif on Japanese porcelains during the third quarter of the seventeenth century.[19]

Shards of dishes similar to figures 27 and 28 have been excavated at the Nangawara and Chokichidani kiln sites and may represent early products of the Kakiemon workshop.[20]

Fig. 28
DISH WITH DOUBLE PEACH DESIGN
Japan, Arita, c. 1660–70
D: 21 cm

JAPANESE PORCELAIN:
EARLY OVERGLAZE ENAMELLED WARES

Detail of fig. 35.

ENAMELS ARE BASICALLY POWDERED GLASS coloured with metallic oxides and mixed with a binding agent to make a paste that can be painted onto metal, glass or ceramic objects. When the objects are fired in a special double-walled kiln called a "muffle kiln" to a temperature in the range of 600–850 degrees Celsius, the enamels melt and adhere to the surface, creating a colourful design.

The application of enamels to ceramics may have started in Iran during the twelfth century and was known in China by the thirteenth century. Porcelain enamelling began in China in the fifteenth century but did not become widely popular there until the sixteenth century.[21] Over time, Chinese enamellers developed a broad palette of colours that included red, yellow, green, turquoise, aubergine and black. These colours were often used in conjunction with underglaze blue to create rich polychromatic designs.

The knowledge of porcelain enamelling probably spread from China to Japan in the 1640s and may have been brought by potters fleeing the turmoil that accompanied the fall of the Ming dynasty. Some influences may also have come to Arita from Kyoto, where a potter named Nonomura Ninsei was developing a style of enamelled earthenware at around the same time.[22]

Wherever the enamelling technique came from, Japanese porcelain decorators soon made it their own. They developed their own colours (including a cobalt-blue enamel that did not become common in China until much later) and used the enamels in different ways to create different types of designs. As both domestic and foreign demand for Japanese porcelain increased in the second half of the seventeenth century, enamelled wares gradually became the most important focus of the industry.

Fig. 29
MODEL OF A TORTOISE
Japan, Arita, c. 1660–70
L: 16.5 cm G04.18.46

Early Japanese porcelain enamels were typically rather dark and opaque, and as the objects illustrated here demonstrate, they were used to decorate a wide variety of both functional and decorative forms.[23]

The model of the tortoise looks like a decorative sculpture, but a hole in the middle of its back suggests that it may have functioned as a base for something else. Japanese mythology held that some tortoises could live for ten thousand years, and artists often depicted these ancient tortoises with waterweeds hanging from their shells. Europeans mistook the waterweeds for flames, with the result that this type of sculpture came to be known in Europe as a "flaming tortoise."[24]

Burning incense was a common practice in seventeenth-century Japan. It was done partly for aesthetic reasons, to enjoy the pleasant scent, but also for practical reasons, to mask the bad odours that could be a real problem in crowded urban environments.[25] The incense burner shown here would have been used in a private Japanese home. A layer of sand would have been placed in the interior to protect the body from the hot incense coals, and the mouth would have been fitted with a silver mesh cover to help diffuse the smoke. Cranes and tortoises were both symbols of longevity in traditional Japanese culture and appear together frequently on seventeenth- and eighteenth-century porcelains.

The enamel colours used on the bowl are similar to the colours found on some Chinese ceramics that were exported to Southeast Asia and the Islamic world in the sixteenth and early seventeenth centuries.[26] It is possible this bowl was also made for export, though the image of pine and bamboo is more in keeping with native Japanese tastes.

Fig. 30
INCENSE BURNER WITH CRANE AND TORTOISE DESIGN
Japan, Arita, c. 1660–70
H: 7.8 cm

Fig. 31
BOWL WITH PINE AND BAMBOO DESIGN
Japan, Arita, c. 1660–70
D: 15.5 cm G04.18.36

Fig. 32
SMALL JAR WITH BIRD AND FLOWER DESIGN
Japan, Arita, c. 1670–80
H: 14.1 cm

Fig. 33
PAIR OF SMALL JARS WITH FLORAL DESIGNS
Japan, Arita, c. 1660
H: 13.2 cm G04.18.34.1-2

TWO DISHES WITH *KRAAK* DESIGNS
Japan, Arita, c. 1660–70
D: 30.8 and 20 cm G05.12.14-15

from carrack, a type of Portuguese ship.[27] In the sixteenth century, Portuguese traders were the first to bring a new kind of Chinese porcelain to Europe that featured a central panel with a landscape scene and a compartmented border filled with flowers and auspicious symbols. When the Ming dynasty fell in 1644, the resulting struggle for power led to a sharp decrease in Chinese porcelain exports. Dutch traders made up for this shortfall by placing orders with the newly established porcelain factories in Japan. The Japanese decorators initially copied Chinese *kraak* designs quite their own distinct versions.[28]

Small jars were another staple of the export trade, though they were used within Japan as well. The dense, energetic bird and flower design on the single jar illustrated here appears only on jars of this form and almost certainly represents the work of an individual enamelling workshop.[29] The pair of jars is also unusual for mixing underglaze cobalt blue with overglaze enamels in a way that is more typically Chinese than Japanese.[30]

Fig. 35
LARGE JAR WITH LANDSCAPE DESIGN
Japan, Arita, c. 1660
H: 26.5 cm G04.18.33

The ability to use colour inspired some Japanese porcelain decorators to attempt more complex, painterly designs on their wares. For example, the landscape on the large jar illustrated above is reminiscent of the Chinese-influenced Kano school of painting.[31] The Kano tradition was particularly associated with the samurai class during the seventeenth and eighteenth centuries and was used by porcelain decorators to create works for both the domestic and export markets. The surface of this jar is marred by several large craters where air bubbles burst and broke off chunks of clay during the firing process. Such damage would normally consign a piece to the shard pile, but the demand for Japanese porcelain was so great in the mid- to late seventeenth century that even flawed pieces like this jar were decorated and sold.[32]

The second jar is decorated with an image of a garden as viewed from a wooden veranda. The style of painting is close to that of the Tosa school, and similar scenes can be found on contemporary Tosa screen paintings.[33] The subject recalls aristocratic poetry and tales of courtly life and indicates that this jar may have been made for the Kyoto market where Tosa painting was especially popular. Similar jars in other museum and private collections are probably products of the same workshop.[34]

Fig. 36

LARGE JAR WITH GARDEN DESIGN

Japan, Arita, c. 1660

H: 24.7 cm

JAPANESE PORCELAIN: **KO-KUTANI, NABESHIMA AND IMARI WARES**

Detail of fig. 52.

THE EXPANSION OF JAPAN'S PORCELAIN INDUSTRY in the second half of the seventeenth century was accompanied by the emergence of several distinct decorative styles. The development of these styles was partly a result of artistic inspiration and partly a result of commercial pressure. As demand for Japanese porcelain increased and a more diverse assortment of buyers (Japanese, Chinese and Dutch) entered the marketplace, the porcelain makers had to develop more distinctive products to attract business and to suit the different tastes and lifestyles of their customers.

The characteristics of the three styles illustrated in this section were discussed in the introductory essays and do not need to be reviewed here. However, a word should be said about nomenclature. Many of the names that are now used to describe different stylistic categories of Japanese porcelain have confusing origins and can sometimes hinder understanding of the objects more than they help it.[35] The name Ko-Kutani is a case in point. Ko-Kutani literally means "old Kutani," and for years it was taken to mean that Ko-Kutani pieces were made at the Kutani kilns in Kaga prefecture on the main island of Honshu. But archaeological evidence gathered between the 1970s and 1990s has shown that most or all of the wares we call Ko-Kutani were actually made in the Arita factories on Kyushu.[36] One possible explanation for this confusion may be that the name Ko-Kutani was retroactively applied. In the 1820s, a factory near Kutani did begin making porcelains that imitated the style we now call Ko-Kutani. People at the time may have assumed that this factory was continuing or reviving a local porcelain tradition and thus incorrectly used the name Ko-Kutani to describe the prototype wares. In any case, Ko-Kutani is now the generally accepted term, but it and other style names like Matsugatani, Imari and Kakiemon must be used cautiously with the understanding that the groups of objects they refer to may contain as many differences as similarities.

Fig. 37
DISH WITH BIRD AND FLOWER DESIGN
Japan, Arita, c. 1640–50
D: 19.7 cm

The Ko-Kutani style included several distinct sub-styles. One important sub-style was the *gosaide,* or "five-colour" style. The name comes from the Japanese pronunciation of the Chinese term *wucai* that was used to describe the palette of porcelain enamels popular in China at the end of the Ming dynasty. *Gosaide* Ko-Kutani wares are typically decorated with Chinese-inspired designs such as the bird and flower image on this dish, which also appears on a nearly identical dish in a Japanese collection.[37]

DISH WITH BANANA-LEAF DESIGN
Japan, Arita, c. 1650
D: 24.1 cm

was the *aode,* or "green" style. As the name suggests, *aode* Ko-Kutani wares are often decorated with a deep, translucent green enamel, though yellow, purple and black enamels also feature prominently in this style.[38] *Aode* Ko-Kutani designs are typically very bold and cover the entire surface of the object. The original *aode* style does not middle of the seventeenth century, but it was revived again in the early nineteenth century by potters working at a factory located near the town of Kutani in Kaga prefecture. These revival wares may be the reason why the original wares became known as Ko-Kutani.

Fig. 39
DISH WITH LANDSCAPE DESIGN
Japan, Arita, 1650–70
D: 25.5 cm

In the 1620s, a publisher in China produced a set of woodcut-illustrated books called *Manuals on Eight Kinds of Painting* (in Chinese, *Bazhong huapu;* in Japanese, *Hasshu gafu*) that were designed to teach people about the basic subjects and styles of Chinese painting.[39] These painting manuals were brought to Japan sometime around the middle of the seventeenth century and immediately had a huge impact there, providing models for thousands of artists and decorators who wanted to create works in Chinese styles but had limited access to original Chinese objects. The landscape image on this dish is typical of the designs that were inspired by the imported Chinese books. This kind of dissemination of information through woodblock-printed books was a critical factor in the larger evolution of Japanese culture during the seventeenth and eighteenth centuries. The back of the dish is painted with an unusual mark reading *homare,* or "esteemed" (see detail on p. 193).

Fig. 40
FLASK WITH SPIRAL DESIGN
Japan, Arita, c. 1650–60
H: 15.5 cm

Fig. 41
WASTE BOWL
Japan, Arita, c. 1650–60
D: 21.5 cm

Food dishes were the most common Ko-Kutani forms, but the style was used to decorate other forms as well. The waste bowl (used for tea dregs) is a relatively rare form based on a Chinese prototype called a *zhadou*.[40] It is decorated with a Ming-style floral design and is inscribed with an apocryphal Ming-dynasty reign mark from the Jiajing period (1521–67).[41] The flask was also inspired by a Chinese model.[42] Its undulating form represents a calabash gourd, a traditional symbol of immortality in Daoism.

Both of these objects show signs of having been damaged and repaired. The waste bowl was broken into several pieces at some point and glued back together with gold and silver lacquer. The flask originally had a longer neck that must have broken and later been cut down to its present height.[43] The care that was taken to preserve these objects even when they were damaged indicates how highly porcelains were valued in traditional Japanese culture.

Fig. 42
SMALL DISH WITH MELON DESIGN
Japan, Arita, c. 1650
L: 17.9 cm

Another distinct style of enamel decoration that emerged in the 1650s is the so-called Matsugatani style. Matsugatani was the name of a village in Saga prefecture, but it is not clear what connection, if any, that village had to these porcelains. Compared with the heavily Chinese-influenced Ko-Kutani style, Matsugatani wares exhibit a much more Japanese aesthetic sensibility, with highly stylized, asymmetrical designs and a much lighter colour palette.[44] The Matsugatani style appears mainly on small, irregularly shaped food dishes of the type that were used in tea ceremony meals. There are numerous formal and design similarities between Matsugatani wares and later Nabeshima wares, leading some experts to think that the Nabeshima factory may originally have been staffed with potters and decorators taken from the workshops that produced the Matsugatani style.

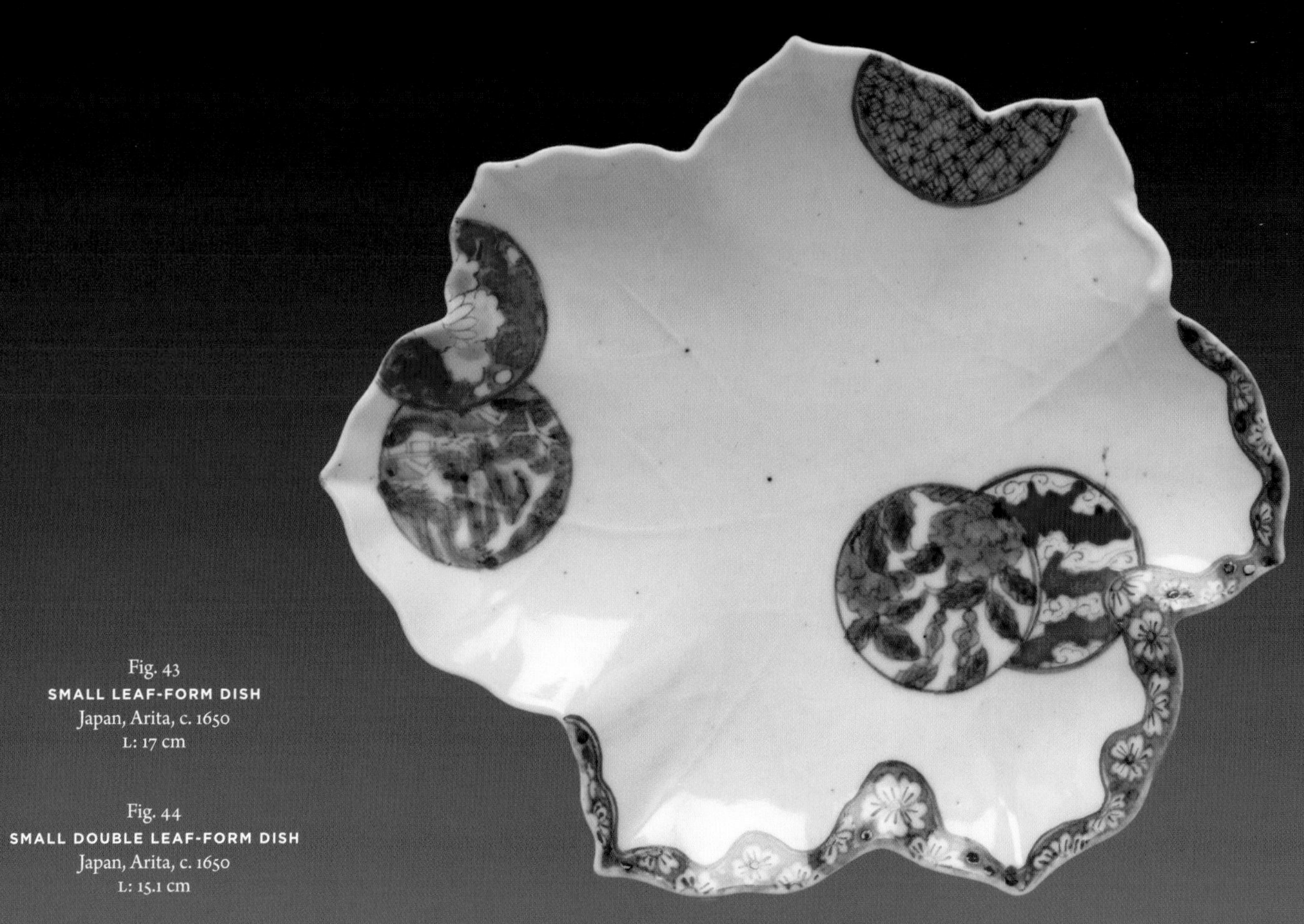

Fig. 43
SMALL LEAF-FORM DISH
Japan, Arita, c. 1650
L: 17 cm

Fig. 44
SMALL DOUBLE LEAF-FORM DISH
Japan, Arita, c. 1650
L: 15.1 cm

Fig. 45
NABESHIMA DISH WITH MISTY BAMBOO DESIGN
Japan, Okawachi, c. 1680–1700
D: 14.9 cm

Nabeshima dishes are famous for the quality of their potting and decoration. The designs on Nabeshima wares are often highly evocative, recalling images from classical Japanese literature and painting.[45] This dish, with its image of a bamboo grove infused by bands of mist, is a prime example. The carefully arranged contrasts between the light-blue bamboo stalks, dark-blue bamboo leaves and white patches of mist successfully convey a sense of depth, texture and atmosphere.

The Nabeshima factory produced mainly small round dishes in a range of standardized sizes, though it also produced some irregularly shaped dishes and non-dish forms.[46] Fragments of Nabeshima wares have been excavated at the sites of several daimyo residences, suggesting that the products of the factory circulated quite widely among the military elite class.[47]

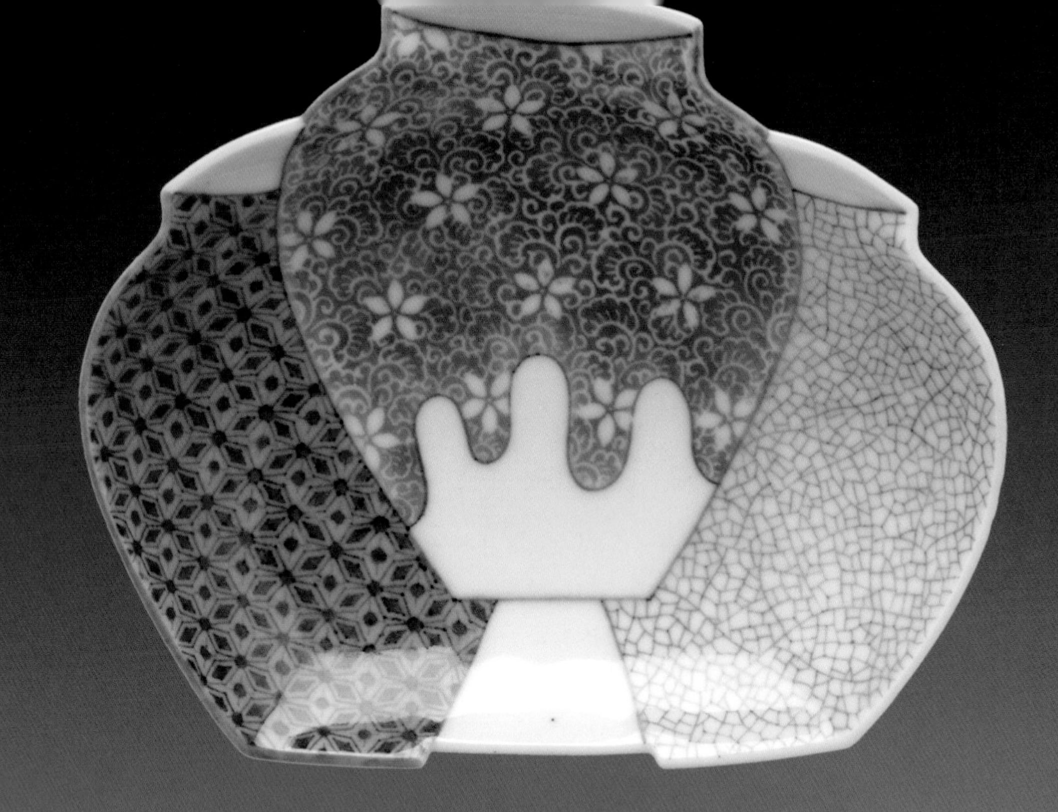

Fig. 46
NABESHIMA DISH WITH WINE JAR DESIGN
Japan, Okawachi, c. 1680–1720
W: 14 cm

Fig. 47
NABESHIMA DISH WITH HYDRANGEA DESIGN
Japan, Okawachi, c. 1680–1720
D: 14.8 cm

Dense, colourful designs, such as the one on this flask, became characteristic of the Imari style. The dynamic image of sinuous water plantains set against a background of vertical lines and scattered prunus blossoms would have required careful planning and tremendous control of the brush to execute. A similar flask is in the collection of the Kyushu Ceramic Museum.[48]

Fig. 48
KO-IMARI FLASK
Japan, Arita, c. 1660
H: 25 cm

Fig. 49
CENSER IN THE FORM OF A CRICKET CAGE
Japan, Arita, c. 1660–80
H: 8.6 cm

Burning fine incense was a mark of wealth and refinement in seventeenth- and eighteenth-century Japan. Connoisseurs sought out incense made from unusual substances and sometimes held playful competitions to identify rare scents.[49] Keeping crickets to enjoy their "music" was another elegant, upper-class pastime. This small censer in the shape of a cricket cage refers to both activities and would thus have been doubly effective as a status symbol to people of the period. The censer belongs to a recognized group that may all have come from the same workshop.[50]

Fig. 30
DISH WITH CRANE AND POND DESIGN
China, Jingdezhen, c. 1620–40
W: 21.5 cm
DISH WITH CRANE AND POND DESIGN
Japan, Arita, c. 1700
W: 34 cm

Chinese potters of the late Ming period produced porcelains in a range of different styles for the Japanese market. The dish below on the left is an example of the most lavish style from that time.[51] It features a design of water birds in a pond, surrounded by various aquatic creatures on the rim. The production of these dishes ceased with the collapse of the Ming dynasty in 1644, but the demand for them in Japan must have continued because they were imitated by Japanese potters at the end of the seventeenth and beginning of the eighteenth centuries. As the dish below on the right demonstrates, the reproductions were often quite faithful to the originals in design, if not always in size. Dishes such as these were not common and may have been made for a very specific market.[52]

Fig. 51
PLATE WITH IMAGE OF FIGHTING CENTAURS
Japan, Arita, c. 1700–20
D: 26.5 cm

Centaurs were creatures from ancient Greek mythology. Half human and half horse, they were supposedly prone to violence and often fought among themselves and with others, using clubs and swords as weapons. A number of artists in Europe during the sixteenth and seventeenth centuries created images of battling centaurs, inspired by various classical stories. The exact source of the image depicted on this plate has not yet been identified, but it was probably taken from a Western engraving sent to Japan specifically to be copied onto porcelains for the export trade. Two other versions of this plate that must have been created in the same workshop exist in the collections of the Kyushu Ceramic Museum and Idemitsu Museum in Japan.[53]

Fig. 52
MODEL OF A PUPPY
Japan, Arita, c. 1680
L: 23.9 cm

Japanese porcelain workshops began producing ornamental sculptures at least as early as the middle of the seventeenth century.[54] Somewhat similar to *okimono* carvings, these sculptures may have been made initially for the domestic market as lighthearted playthings to be included in certain types of holiday and other seasonal displays.[55] But as soon as the sculptures came to the attention of Dutch and Chinese buyers, they became popular export products as well, and by the end of the seventeenth century, foreign consumption of the sculptures may actually have eclipsed domestic consumption.

The animal figures illustrated here are all symbols of certain years in the traditional Chinese and Japanese zodiac and could have been used within Japan as gifts or decorations for the New Year's festival.[56] If so, they would likely have been stored away once the festivities were over. In Europe, by contrast, animal sculptures such as these were seen simply as charming nature studies and were often left on display all year.

Fig. 53
MODEL OF A RABBIT
Japan, Arita, c. 1700
H: 20.5 cm

Fig. 54
MODEL OF A COCKEREL
Japan, Arita, c. 1700–20
L: 19.3 cm G05.11.16

JAPANESE PORCELAIN: **KAKIEMON WARES**

Fig. 55
DISH WITH BIRD ON A FLOWERING BRANCH
Japan, Arita, c. 1670
D: 21.6 cm G05.12.16

AS OLIVER IMPEY'S ESSAY EXPLAINS, the Kakiemon style developed sometime around the 1660s or 70s at least partly in response to the growing foreign demand for Japanese porcelain. Indeed, Impey suggests that the Kakiemon style may have emerged primarily to cater to the tastes of Chinese merchants, whereas the Imari style may have evolved primarily to cater to the tastes of Dutch merchants.[57] Although there may be some truth to this hypothesis, it does not account for the influence of Japanese consumers who were also major buyers of Arita porcelain. When their tastes are factored into the equation, the development of Kakiemon and other seventeenth-century styles looks more like a complex response to a competitive market in which various workshops were attempting to create porcelains with different combinations of Japanese, Chinese and Western elements to suit the tastes of multiple audiences.

Whatever the origins of the Kakiemon style were, it became extremely popular among porcelain makers and consumers in both Japan and Europe during the late seventeenth and early eighteenth centuries. In Japan, shards of Kakiemon wares have been found at a number of archaeological sites, indicating that it was appreciated and used by at least some wealthy Japanese of that time.[58] In Europe, Kakiemon wares commanded higher prices than any other type of Asian porcelain and later became a major source of inspiration for many Western porcelain decorators. The classic Kakiemon style seems to have disappeared in Japan for several decades following the decline of the export trade in the 1730s, but it was revived in the nineteenth century and is still being produced today.

Fig. 36
DISH WITH CHERRY BLOSSOMS AND CHRYSANTHEMUM
Japan, Arita, c. 1670–90
D: 22.9 cm G07.18.15

These objects are all examples of Kakiemon wares that might have been made for the domestic Japanese market. The dish, for instance, might have been used for serving a whole fish or some type of stew at a festive banquet.[59] It is decorated with seasonal flowers that were associated with spring and autumn in traditional Japanese culture. An apocryphal Ming-dynasty reign mark on the back would have appealed to Japanese connoisseurs of the period (see a detail of the mark on p. 193).

Fig. 57
FOOD TRAY
Japan, Arita, c. 1690–1700
D: 15 cm

Fig. 58
KETTLE
Japan, Arita, c. 1670–90
L: 19.4 cm

The food tray originally had additional trays and a lid stacked on top to create a multi-tiered box.[60] It would have been used for serving several different courses of a meal to a single diner or small dining party. It is decorated with scenes of classical Japanese court figures inspired by the Yamato-e painting tradition.[61]

Based on a traditional lacquer form, the kettle would most likely have been used for serving warm rice wine.[62] It is decorated with birds of prey and auspicious fruits arranged to create crest-like designs that would have appealed to members of the samurai class.

Although pieces like these may have been made for the domestic market originally, they were also exported. Domestic wares were sometimes added to make up shortfalls in export orders, and if those pieces proved to be popular with foreign consumers, they became regular export products as well.

Fig. 59
FIGURE OF BOY SITTING ON A DRUM
Japan, Arita, c. 1670–80
H: 14 cm G05.12.24

Fig. 60
PAIR OF SMALL FEMALE FIGURES
Japan, Arita, c. 1670–90
H: 14.5 cm G05.12.25.1-2

Along with ornamental animal figures, the Arita workshops also produced a variety of ornamental human figures. These figures were typically drawn from popular culture and included folk deities, legendary heroes and characters from the entertainment world.[63] The sculptures were made using press-moulds that produced multiple identical copies of each figure. The identical figures were then sometimes made more individual by painting them with different colours and clothing designs.

The sculptures illustrated here represent two common types of Kakiemon figure. The figure of the boy sitting on a drum and carrying a calabash gourd on his back may represent a Chinese Daoist immortal or possibly an entertainer from the Kabuki theatre.[64] The female figures represent a category known generically as *bijin,* or "beautiful women." Inspired by glamorous courtesans and female-impersonating Kabuki actors, *bijin* figures were also depicted in scroll paintings and prints of the same period.[65] The figures may originally have been made to decorate teahouses and brothels in Japan's big cities or to be paraded around the entertainment districts on certain festival days.

Human figures in porcelain quickly caught the attention of foreign merchants and were exported to the West in significant quantities during the late seventeenth century. Because they were highly valued by Western collectors, the figures have tended to survive better there than in Japan. But as the dated Kakiemon moulds discussed in Oliver Impey's essay prove, human figure sculptures continued to be made for the Japanese domestic market throughout the eighteenth and nineteenth centuries.

Fig. 61
LARGE FEMALE FIGURE
Japan, Arita, c. 1680
H: 31.5 cm G07.18.1

Fig. 62
SMALL INCENSE BURNER WITH LION FINIAL
Japan, Arita, c. 1700–20
H: 10.9 cm G05.12.23

Fig. 63
FLOWER BASKET WITH EUROPEAN METAL MOUNTS
Japan, Arita, c. 1690–1710
H: 12 cm

Fig. 64
DISH WITH PINES AND BOATS
Japan, Arita, c. 1680–1700
D: 17.5 cm

This rare dish is an example of Kakiemon ware at its finest.[66] It is painted with a highly stylized design of pine-covered islands and boats at sea that almost certainly represents the scenery of Matsushima Bay. Located in Miyagi prefecture on the northern coast of Honshu, Matsushima Bay has long been one of Japan's most famous scenic spots and was celebrated in several famous seventeenth-century poems and paintings, including a screen painting by the artist Tawaraya Sotatsu, whose simplified, lyrical style is evoked on this dish.[67]

The milky white body of the dish is called *nigoshide* in Japanese and was especially associated with the Kakiemon workshop during the seventeenth century.[68] *Nigoshide* dishes were made from the same basic clay as other Arita porcelains, but *nigoshide* clay underwent extra washing and refining steps to remove all trace impurities, resulting in a brilliant white surface for decoration.

In the Chinese language, the word for "quail" *(an)* sounds like the word for "peace," so Chinese artists often depicted quails to convey a wish for peace and harmony.[69] The quail motif spread from China to Japan sometime around the fourteenth century and was transformed there into a symbol for autumn as well.[70] Seasonal imagery was very important in traditional Japanese culture and many upper-class households changed their furnishings to reflect the different times of year. The Arita dish illustrated here may once have belonged to a larger set that was specifically intended to be used in autumn.[71]

Fig. 65
DISH WITH QUAIL AND MILLET
Japan, Arita, c. 1670–90
D: 15.1 cm G04.18.37

Fig. 66
PLATE WITH QUAIL DESIGN
China, Jingdezhen, c. 1740–50
D: 23 cm G05.12.1

Fig. 67
DECAGONAL DISH WITH TIGER, PRUNUS AND BAMBOO
Japan, Arita, c. 1680–1700
W: 22 cm
DECAGONAL DISH WITH TIGER, PRUNUS AND BAMBOO
Japan, Arita, c. 1690–1710
W: 15.5 cm G05.11.15

Kakiemon wares were produced in different levels of quality, as the two dishes shown below demonstrate. Although the dishes have the same basic form and design, one (on the left) has a *nigoshide* body, whereas the other does not. The *nigoshide* dish also has a richly coloured landscape surrounding the tiger, whereas the other dish has a simpler setting. The existence of different quality levels indicates just how responsive to market pressures the Japanese porcelain industry had become by the end of the seventeenth century. As was seen in the section on early blue and white wares, the combination of tiger and bamboo was a traditional Japanese art motif, but both of these dishes were most likely made for the European market.[72]

Fig. 68
DECAGONAL PLATE WITH PHOENIX DESIGN
Japan, Arita, c. 1690–1700
W: 23.1 cm
DECAGONAL PLATE WITH PHOENIX DESIGN
Japan, Arita, c. 1700–20
W: 19.2 cm

Japanese porcelain decorators often used the same basic design motifs over and over again for decades. In some cases, the designs changed very little. In other cases, such as with these dishes, the decorators introduced variations by reversing the composition or changing some specific elements (e.g., the trees) within them.[73]

The brown rim on these and the preceding pair of dishes was copied from Chinese porcelains. In the 1620s and 30s, the Chinese porcelains intended for the Japanese market were often made using poorly prepared clays that shrank too quickly in the kiln and left the glaze around the rim of the dish unsupported and prone to chipping. To mitigate this problem, the Chinese potters sometimes strengthened the rims with an extra coating of iron-oxide glaze.[74] The Japanese came to admire this brown rim and eventually imitated it in their porcelains as a sign of quality.

Fig. 69
OCTAGONAL PLATE WITH SHIBA ONKO DESIGN
Japan, Arita, c. 1680–1700
W: 21 cm

Shiba Onko is the Japanese name for Sima Guang, an eleventh-century Chinese statesman and historian who was greatly revered in both China and Japan. One legend says that as a boy, Shiba saved a playmate from drowning in a large jar of water by breaking the vessel with a rock. The Tokugawa government promoted such stories of loyalty in action, and it is likely that this design was originally created for the domestic market.[75] But because European consumers especially liked figural designs, it was soon adapted for export wares and taken to Europe where it was much copied.[76]

Fig. 70
TEABOWL AND SAUCER WITH DESIGN OF A LADY IN A GARDEN
Japan, Arita, c. 1680–1700
Bowl H: 4 cm; Saucer D: 11.8 cm G05.12.22

The image on this teabowl and saucer of an aristocratic woman standing in a garden is derived from earlier Japanese Yamato-e and Tosa painting traditions.[77] The design (which is sometimes called "The Lady in the Pavilion" in Western sources) recalls numerous poems and stories about young women who yearn for their absent husbands or lovers and who are often kept company only by caged birds. Like the Shiba Onko design, this design was probably made first for the Japanese domestic market before becoming a common motif on wares destined for Europe.[78]

Fig. 71
TWO OCTAGONAL BOWLS WITH THE "THREE FRIENDS OF WINTER" DESIGN
Japan, Arita, c. 1680–1700 and 1690–1710
W: 19.6 cm and 12.6 cm G05.12.20 and G04.18.41

Because they all flourish in cold weather, pine, prunus and bamboo were collectively known as the "Three Friends of Winter" in traditional Chinese and Japanese culture. The Three Friends motif was often used in the visual and decorative arts to symbolize strength and resiliency. Japanese artists developed a special version of the motif in which the bamboo stalks are bound together to form a kind of hedge or fence.[79] This version of the motif, seen on the smaller bowl below, may have been inspired by traditional Japanese gardens, in which hedges and fences were used as important design components.[80] The "banded hedge" design was also frequently copied in Europe, where it was sometimes mistakenly called a wheatsheaf.

Fig. 72
PAIR OF OVOID FLASKS
Japan, Arita, c. 1680–1700
H: 23.3 cm G07.18.10.1-2

During the Tokugawa period, sake rice wine came in different grades and was often served warm as an accompaniment to meals or various forms of entertainment. Traditional sake flasks had relatively thick, pear-shaped bodies and wide, flaring mouths.[81] Porcelain's strength allowed potters to create a new form of sake flask with thinner walls and narrower mouths. The new flask form was highly practical because the narrow neck helped to preserve the alcohol's heat and made it easier to pour into the small cups used to drink sake. Pairs of sake flasks were often exported to Europe in the seventeenth and eighteenth centuries where they were admired as decorative objects.

Fig. 73
PAIR OF SQUARE FLASKS
Japan, Arita, c. 1680–1700
H: 26 cm G07.18.13.1-2

Fig. 74
PAIR OF HEXAGONAL FLASKS
Japan, Arita, c. 1680–1700
H: 22.9 cm G07.18.14.1-2

Two types of tea were popular in Japan during the seventeenth and eighteenth centuries. *Matcha* was powdered green tea that was combined with hot water in a medium-sized bowl and whipped into a froth with a bamboo whisk; this type of tea was used in the tea ceremony. *Sencha* was green tea in leaf form that was steeped in a small pot and served in small bowls or cups. Because it was easier to prepare and did not require so much ceremony, *sencha* became the preferred beverage of many urban artists and poets during the Tokugawa period.[82]

The teapot and teabowls illustrated here would have been used for serving *sencha*. The design of the saucers that accompany the teabowls is sometimes called the "snowflake" design because of their delicately scrolling edges. Large quantities of teapots and teabowls were also exported to Europe where tea drinking was a newly fashionable practice in the seventeenth century.

Fig. 75
HEXAGONAL TEAPOT
Japan, Arita, c. 1670–90
L: 10.5 cm

Fig. 76
PAIR OF TEABOWLS AND SAUCERS
Japan, Arita, c. 1660–80
Bowl H: 4 cm; Saucer D: 11 cm G04.18.38.1-2

Fig. 77
COVERED CENSER
Japan, Arita, c. 1680–1700
W: 17.9 cm G05.11.14

As has already been discussed, many Japanese porcelains originally made for the domestic market ended up in export shipments to Europe where they assumed new functions and meanings. This covered tripod vessel is a good example. In Japan, vessels of this shape were used for burning incense; when they were exported to Europe, they became serving dishes for richly spiced stews.[83]

Some porcelain forms were made exclusively for the export market. The mug and two ewers are examples of this category. Their forms were copied from wooden or ceramic models supplied by Dutch merchants for the Japanese potters to copy, and they are decorated with Europeanized floral designs.[84] For the most part, wares such as these did not have much impact within Japan.

Fig. 78
BELL-SHAPED MUG
Japan, Arita, c. 1670–90
H: 11.1 cm G05.12.17
PAIR OF STRAP-HANDLE EWERS
Japan, Arita, c. 1670–90
H: 14.5 cm G04.18.35.1-2

Fig. 79
PLATE WITH UNDERGLAZE LANDSCAPE DESIGN
Japan, Arita, c. 1680–1700
D: 23.2 cm G04.18.43

Fig. 80
BOWL WITH PINES AND BOATS
Japan, Arita, c. 1690–1710
W: 13.5 cm

Although the Kakiemon style is most closely associated with polychrome enamel wares, a blue and white version of the style also existed. Produced primarily for the domestic market, blue and white Kakiemon wares typically feature carefully painted pictorial designs. This bowl is an unusually fine example of Kakiemon blue and white. It is decorated with an image of pine-clad islands and boats in Matsushima Bay that is similar to the image on the enamel-decorated dish illustrated earlier in this section (fig. 64).[85]

The two dishes illustrated on the next page are also examples of Kakiemon blue and white wares. One is decorated with a simple garden design similar to images seen in some paintings made for the tea ceremony. It is inscribed on the reverse with the character *kin,* meaning "gold," which also appears on a number of other Kakiemon porcelains from the same period. (See p. 193 for a detail of the mark on fig. 81.) The second dish is decorated with an image of deer and pine trees, which together signify a wish for prosperity and long life in traditional Chinese and Japanese art.

Fig. 81
PLATE WITH FLOWER AND FENCE DESIGN
Japan, Arita, c. 1680
D: 18.5 cm

Fig. 82
PLATE WITH DEER AND PINE DESIGN
Japan, Arita, c. 1680–1700
D: 21.5 cm

Fig. 83
DISH WITH PRUNUS AND BAMBOO
Japan, Arita, c. 1690–1710
D: 19 cm G05.12.21

THE JAPANESE STYLE IN EUROPE: **THE NETHERLANDS**

Fig. 84
PLATE WITH BAMBOO AND PRUNUS DESIGN
The Netherlands, Delft, c. 1700–30
Marked AVK. D: 20 cm G04.18.32

THE DUTCH EAST INDIA COMPANY was formed in 1602 to manage the Netherlands' business relations in Asia and quickly became a powerful force in the European trade with China.[86] In 1639, the Company's position in Asia was further strengthened when the Tokugawa government imposed a partial "closed door" policy that allowed only Chinese, Korean and Dutch merchants to trade directly with Japan. The Dutch merchants were confined to a small island in Nagasaki harbour, and their activities were closely monitored by the Japanese authorities. But even with those limitations, the Japan trade was still enormously profitable for the Dutch, especially after Chinese exports to Europe fell sharply in the late 1640s. By the 1660s, the Netherlands had become the major hub in Europe for the trade in all things Asian, including porcelains.

The tremendous flow of Chinese, and later Japanese, porcelains into the Netherlands during the seventeenth century inevitably had a major impact on the native Dutch ceramics industry.[87] Although the Dutch did not know the formula for making true porcelain, they devised new varieties of tin-glazed earthenware that more closely imitated the appearance of Asian porcelain. Moreover, in the early eighteenth century, some Dutch artists developed sideline businesses adding their own overglaze enamel decoration to porcelain blanks imported from Asia. Most of the Asian-style Dutch ceramics produced in the seventeenth and eighteenth centuries followed Chinese models, but Japanese-style ceramics were also popular between the 1700s and 1740s. At that time, the best Japanese porcelains were commanding huge prices in Europe, so the Dutch imitation wares found a ready market among middle-class consumers who could not afford the real things.

Fig. 85
OVAL BASIN
The Netherlands, Delft, c. 1720–30
Marked AR. W: 23 cm

Sometime around the ninth or tenth century, potters in the Islamic world discovered that the addition of tin oxide could opacify a standard lead glaze and create a bright white ground that approximated the look of porcelain.[88] Knowledge of this glazing technique spread from the Islamic world to southern Europe in the thirteenth and fourteenth centuries, and from southern Europe to northern Europe in the sixteenth and seventeenth centuries. Dutch potters whose industry was at that time being squeezed by a flood of imports from China and Japan successfully used the technique to create earthenware vessels that at least superficially resembled porcelains.

Dutch potters began imitating Japanese porcelain designs on a large scale in the early 1700s. By modifying the designs and applying them to European vessel forms, the Dutch potters created a new, hybrid form of ceramic art. The oval basin shown here is a good example. The exterior of the basin is decorated with Japanese-inspired images of cranes, banded hedges, cherry blossoms and chrysanthemums, whereas its interior is decorated with a European floral bouquet. The basin's form is entirely European and may have been used for cooling wine bottles at the dinner table.[89]

Fig. 86
PLATE WITH DRAGON AND FOX DESIGN
The Netherlands, Delft, c. 1720–30
Marked AR. D: 22.2 cm

The design on this dinner plate was clearly inspired by the traditional Japanese dragon and tiger motif. However, the decorator seems not to have recognized the tiger in the original and so transformed it into a fox on this copy.[90]

This dish and the basin on the preceding page both bear the monogram of a well-known decorator named Ary van Rijsselberg.[91] (A detail of the plate's monogram mark is illustrated on p. 193.) Van Rijsselberg first worked at a Delft pottery called De Grieksche A (The Greek A) from around 1713 to 1718. Later, from 1718 to 1735, he worked at another pottery called De Drie Vergulde Astonnekens (The Three Cinder Tubs). He seems to have specialized in Japanese-style designs. Objects with van Rijsselberg's monogram are numerous and vary in style, so some scholars think a portion of his signed work may have been done by apprentices or journeymen decorators working under his supervision.

top, Fig. 87
PAIR OF BUTTER DISHES
The Netherlands, Delft, c. 1740
W: 12.8 cm G05.11.2.1-2

bottom, Fig. 88
TEAPOT WITH BANDED HEDGE AND BIRD DESIGN
The Netherlands, Delft, c. 1720–30
L: 21.3 cm G07.18.09
TEAPOT WITH FLORAL DESIGN
The Netherlands, Delft, c. 1740
L: 15.3 cm

Fig. 89
DISH WITH SHIBA ONKO DESIGN
The Netherlands, Delft, c. 1740
Marked AK. D: 30.5 cm

The Shiba Onko design was first copied in Europe at the Meissen factory in Saxony around 1730 and was quickly imitated by decorators in many other countries across Europe. Most of the decorators were probably unfamiliar with the story behind the design and consequently did not always get the details of the image exactly right. On this dish, for instance, the birds flying around the trees in the original (see fig. 69) are replaced by floating flowers, and the water spilling from the broken jar is replaced by odd, cloud-like billows. The reverse of the dish bears the monogram of Adriaen Kocks, master of *De Grieksche A* pottery from 1687 to 1701, but the mark is spurious and the dish was actually painted by another unidentified artist several decades after Kocks's death.[92]

Fig. 90
PLATE WITH CRANE AND FLOWERING TREE
Chinese porcelain, c. 1700–20
decorated in the Netherlands, c. 1710–30
D: 21 cm G04.18.01

In addition to decorating their own ceramics in the Japanese style, Dutch potters also painted Japanese designs on porcelain blanks acquired from China or from the Meissen factory in Saxony.[93] The images on these pieces range from faithful imitations of Japanese originals to more eclectic designs that combine various Japanese, Chinese and Western elements. This plate is a good example of the second category. The basic design is Japanese, whereas the depiction of the tree with its oversize blossoms comes from Chinese porcelains, and the symmetry of the composition and the placement of the design in the middle of the dish are more European. Although the design contains a mix of influences, the painting is extremely fine and was clearly done by a highly accomplished artist. An inscribed number on the bottom of the plate indicates that it once belonged to the Saxon royal collection.[94]

Fig. 91
SCALLOPED PLATE WITH BOY AND TIGERS
Chinese porcelain, c. 1700–20
decorated in China or the Netherlands, c. 1720
D: 24.9 cm

Fig. 92
PAIR OF TEA CADDIES
Chinese porcelain, c. 1725
decorated in the Netherlands, c. 1730
H: 11.2 cm

Fig. 93
BEAKER WITH SHIBA ONKO DESIGN
Chinese porcelain, c. 1700–20
decorated in the Netherlands, c. 1730
H: 6.7 cm

THE JAPANESE STYLE IN EUROPE: **GERMANY**

Fig. 94
SCALLOPED BOWL WITH BIRD ON A FLOWERING BRANCH
Meissen porcelain, c. 1720
decorated in the Netherlands, c. 1725–30
W: 17.3 cm

JUST AS AN UNSATISFIED DEMAND for Chinese porcelain stimulated the development of the porcelain industry in Japan, so too did an unsatisfied demand lead to the production of porcelain in Europe. Potters in many European countries experimented with different recipes for making porcelain in the late sixteenth and seventeenth centuries.[95] Some of those attempts in Italy and France succeeded in creating new types of ceramics that resembled porcelain, but the first successful production of true porcelain was achieved in the German state of Saxony by two scientists, Ehrenfried Walther von Tschirnhaus and Johann Friedrich Böttger, working for the Saxon ruler, Augustus II, also known as Augustus the Strong. Böttger presented the formula for porcelain to Augustus in March 1709. (Tschirnhaus had died in 1708.) Starting in 1710, Böttger headed the first porcelain factory at Meissen near the Saxon capital of Dresden.[96]

During its first decade of operation, the Meissen factory produced mainly white porcelains with moulded or gilt decoration. Although factory potters experimented with underglaze blue and overglaze enamel decoration, their results were not very successful until a young painter named Johann Gregor Höroldt joined the factory in 1720.[97] Höroldt improved the factory's basic formula for porcelain paste and also developed new recipes and techniques for applying coloured enamel decoration. It was under Höroldt's direction that the Meissen factory first began imitating Japanese porcelain forms and designs in the early 1720s.

Some of the Japanese-inspired wares produced at Meissen were exact copies of Japanese originals; others were various mixtures of Japanese and Western elements. Most of the Japanese-inspired wares made at Meissen between the 1720s and 1750s imitated the Kakiemon style, though some also followed the Imari style. As the first manufacturer of porcelain in Europe, Meissen became a model for many other ceramics factories, and its Japanese-style wares in particular were copied later in numerous different countries.

Fig. 95
SUGAR BOX
Germany, Meissen factory, c. 1723–24
Marked KPM. L: 12.3 cm

At the time this sugar box was made in the early 1720s, the Meissen factory had only just perfected the technique of decorating its porcelains with overglaze enamels. Most of the early overglaze enamel designs used at Meissen were inspired by Chinese porcelains. This is a very early example of a Japanese-influenced design.[98] The drawing and the colouring are still rather crude and may in fact have been applied by an independent deocorator working outside the Meissen factory. Within a few years, however, the Meissen factory was producing copies of Japanese porcelain so exact that they can still be difficult to distinguish from the originals today.

This flask is a good example of a faithful Meissen imitation. It was copied directly from a Japanese flask in the collection of Augustus the Strong.[99] By the 1720s, the Saxon ruler owned several thousand pieces of Chinese and Japanese porcelain, which he made available to the Meissen potters and decorators to study as sources of both forms and designs. Some of the Japanese-style wares made at Meissen were sold as commercial goods in various markets across Europe. Others were retained for Augustus's collection and used in grand displays at the royal palaces. This flask is marked with an inventory number on its base that indicates it once belonged to the Saxon royal collection.[100] (A detail of the mark is illustrated on p. 193.)

Fig. 96
OVOID FLASK
Germany, Meissen factory, c. 1730
H: 21 cm G05.11.5

Fig. 97
HEXAGONAL JAR
Germany, Meissen factory, c. 1730
H: 34.5 cm

Fig. 98
COVERED EWER
Germany, Meissen factory, c. 1731
H: 18.2 cm G04.18.05

One reason Meissen decorators became so skilled at copying Japanese porcelains was a French merchant named Rodolphe Lemaire.[101] In 1728 Lemaire obtained the exclusive right to sell Meissen porcelain in France and the Netherlands. At that time, Japanese Kakiemon porcelain was the most expensive porcelain in Europe. Lemaire wanted to take advantage of this market, so he placed orders for Meissen porcelains that imitated Japanese wares as closely as possible. He further arranged for the pieces that were sent to him to have a special overglaze enamel version of the Meissen factory mark on their bases, instead of the usual underglaze mark. After he received the Meissen porcelains, Lemaire used acid and abrasives to remove the factory marks and sold many of them as Japanese originals for very high prices. Lemaire's fraud was finally revealed in 1731 and his inventory confiscated and returned to Saxony. This ewer has a partially erased Meissen factory mark and may have been one of the pieces involved in the Lemaire scandal.[102]

Fig. 99
SCALLOPED TEABOWL AND SAUCER WITH AMOROUS COUPLE
Germany, Meissen factory, c. 1730
Bowl H: 5.4 cm; Saucer D: 11.5 cm G04.18.04a-b

Fig. 100
SCALLOPED DISH WITH AMOROUS COUPLE
China, Jingdezhen, c. 1700–20
D: 14.3 cm G05.11.01

SCALLOPED TEABOWL AND SAUCER WITH AUSPICIOUS PLANTS
Germany, Meissen factory, c. 1730
Bowl H: 6.6 cm; Saucer D: 15 cm G04.18.03a-b

here were both copied directly from Japanese originals and are decorated with designs derived from traditional Chinese and Japanese sources. The image of the amorous couple, for instance, comes from Chinese paintings and prints of the early seventeenth century and recalls numerous love stories that were popular in Chinese and Japanese drama and literature at the time.[103] The auspicious plants—pomegranate, peony and prunus—also come originally from Chinese art and express wishes for prosperity and good fortune.[104] In Japan, the symbolic meanings of these images would have been

original meanings of the designs were not generally recognized and they were enjoyed simply as ornamental patterns.

As China's porcelain industry resumed large-scale exports to the West in the early eighteenth century, Chinese potters produced imitations of Japanese forms and designs, which they sold to European traders at low prices in an effort to undercut the Japanese export business. The Chinese dish shown here was probably made as part of this early attempt at price warfare.

Fig. 102
MAGNOLIA-FORM TEAPOT
Germany, Meissen factory, c. 1730–40
L: 16.3 cm G04.18.06

In traditional Chinese and Japanese cultures, images of squirrels and grapes together formed a rebus signifying a wish to have many sons.[105] Squirrel and grape images appear in Chinese painting as early as the thirteenth century and in Chinese porcelain as early as the sixteenth century. Japanese decorators began using the design on Kakiemon-style porcelains in the seventeenth century, and it spread to Europe in the eighteenth century.[106] The design was first copied in Europe at the Meissen factory and was imitated later by many other factories in France and England. Because the Europeans did not know the origins of the design, they sometimes mistook the squirrel for a rat and called it the "rat and grape" design.[107]

Meissen decorators used Kakiemon designs to decorate a wide range of porcelain forms, many of which were not Japanese in origin. The form of this teapot, for example, comes from Chinese Yixing earthenware and was probably modelled on a piece in the Saxon royal collection. Only one other Meissen teapot of this shape seems to be recorded.[108]

Fig. 103
TURKISH COFFEE POT
Germany, Meissen factory, c. 1735–40
H: 20.2 cm G07.18.08

Fig. 104
DOUBLE-HANDLED SAUCE BOAT
Germany, Meissen factory, c. 1730–40
L: 21.8 cm G05.12.13

Fig. 105
DOUBLE-HANDLED BASKET
Germany, Meissen factory, c. 1735–40
L: 23.8 cm G04.18.07

Fig. 106
PAIR OF VASES
Germany, Frankenthaler factory, c. 1770
H: 20.5 cm

The Frankenthaler porcelain factory was located in the Palatinate region of south-western Germany. It was founded in 1755 by members of the Hannong family, who had previously worked as ceramics decorators at the Strasbourg factory in France. Frankenthaler is best known for works in the European Rococo style. This pair of vases is an unusual example of Asian-influenced work. The forms of the vases come from Chinese porcelain, except for the fruit finials on the lids that were probably modelled on Meissen wares. The designs on the sides of the vases come from Japanese Kakiemon porcelains, with some additional Chinese elements mixed in. The Frankenthaler factory closed in 1799.

THE JAPANESE STYLE IN EUROPE: **FRANCE**

Fig. 107
SUGAR BOX
France, Saint-Cloud factory, c. 1735–40
H: 10.5 cm G04.18.09

ATTEMPTS TO PRODUCE PORCELAIN IN FRANCE started in the 1660s. In 1664, the Saint-Cloud factory was founded with a mandate to produce both tin-glazed earthenware and Chinese-style porcelain.[109] The earthenware was no problem, but French potters did not know how to make the porcelain. The Saint-Cloud potters experimented with different combinations of materials before finally settling on a paste made largely from a mixture of white clay and crushed glass. This mixture, which was similar to a formula used for many centuries in the Islamic world, is the basic recipe for what is now called "soft-paste" porcelain. The Saint-Cloud factory started producing soft-paste porcelain in the early 1690s and initially created wares with Chinese-inspired designs painted in underglaze blue. It was not until the 1730s that the Saint-Cloud factory began producing porcelains with Japanese-style enamel decoration.

The first French factory to imitate Japanese-style porcelains was the Chantilly factory. The Chantilly factory was founded in the late 1720s by Louis-Henri de Bourbon, the prince de Condé, with help from potters lured away from Saint-Cloud.[110] Like Saint-Cloud, the Chantilly factory produced soft-paste porcelain, but the Chantilly potters used a different glaze formula that was whitened with tin oxide. When this glaze was painted with enamels and fired a second time, it softened and allowed the enamels to sink in, creating a rich, unctuous surface. The prince de Condé owned a large collection of Chinese and Japanese porcelains, which he allowed the decorators at Chantilly to copy. The success of these copies may in turn have inspired the decorators at Saint-Cloud to imitate Japanese designs as well.

The popularity of Japanese-influenced porcelains faded in France after the Sèvres factory emerged as the dominant force in French ceramics during the 1750s. But the end of Japan's "closed door" policy in the middle of the nineteenth century ushered in a new wave of French interest in Japanese art, including the art of porcelain.

The Chantilly factory produced porcelains both for use and for decoration.[111] The snuff box is an example of the factory's functional production. It was used to carry snuff, a mixture of finely ground tobacco and other aromatic plants that was inhaled through the nose as a stimulant and purgative. Snuff-taking was very popular among the French aristocracy during the eighteenth century, and beautifully painted snuff boxes such as this were considered important fashion accessories.[112]

The pair of flasks is an example of Chantilly's decorative production. Although modelled on Japanese sake flasks (see fig. 73, for example), these pieces were made for show rather than for use. A 1740 inventory of the prince de Condé's estate reveals that many Chantilly porcelains were displayed in cabinets around the prince's palace.[113] This pair of flasks is extremely rare and appears to be the only known Chantilly flasks of this form with this decoration.

left, Fig. 108
PAIR OF SQUARE FLASKS
France, Chantilly factory, c. 1730–40
H: 22.3 cm G07.18.07

Fig. 109
SNUFF BOX
France, Chantilly factory, c. 1730–40
L: 6.3 cm

Fig. 110
DEEP BOWL
France, Chantilly factory, c. 1735–45
W: 16.7 cm G05.11.07

This deep bowl might have been used to cool bottles of wine at the table. Although its function is thoroughly European, its form derives from a Japanese bowl.[114] The scrolling floral motif on the outside of the basin may have been based on a Meissen interpretation of a Kakiemon design. Chantilly decorators often copied Meissen designs, as the pieces with the grape and squirrel designs on the opposite page illustrate (compare with fig. 102).

Fig. 111
TEAPOT WITH GRAPE AND SQUIRREL DESIGN
France, Chantilly factory, c. 1730–40
L: 11.9 cm G04.18.10

Fig. 112
PAIR OF WINE BOTTLE COOLERS WITH GRAPE AND SQUIRREL DESIGN
France, Chantilly factory, c. 1730–40
W: 16.7 cm G04.18.13.1-2

Fig. 113
PICKLE DISH
France, Chantilly factory, c. 1730–40
L: 22.4 cm G04.18.11

Fig. 114
PEACH-FORM CUP AND SAUCER
France, Chantilly factory, c. 1730–40
Cup H: 5.9 cm; Saucer W: 14.5 cm G05.12.08

Fig. 11[illegible]

BOTTLE COOLER WITH CHINESE BOYS DESIGN

France, Villeroy factory, c. 1737–48

H: 15.9 cm

[illegible]nded sometime around 1737, the Villeroy factory was sponsored by François-Louis-Anne de Neufville, the duc de Villeroy, and was headed by a potter named François Barbin, who later founded the Mennecy factory.[115] The factory produced wares in both tin-glazed earthenware and soft-paste porcelain. It was a small factory with only fifteen recorded employees, yet it produced wares in an impressive range of forms and decorative styles. Never a great commercial success, however, the factory closed in 1748.

This bottle cooler is a rare example of Villeroy porcelain with a Japanese-influenced design. The theme of young boys playing games came originally from Chinese art and signified the wish to have a large, happy family. The design first appeared on Japanese porcelain in the late seventeenth century and was copied by Meissen, Chantilly and other factories in Europe during the eighteenth century (see figs. 152 and 153).

Samson and Company was founded in the second half of the nineteenth century to reproduce significant pieces of historical porcelain and pottery from museum and private collections in France. At the time, Japan had just ended its "closed door" policy, and there was a new wave of European interest in all things Japanese, including porcelains. Thus, copies of Kakiemon and Kakiemon-inspired Chantilly wares became an important part of the Samson product line. The Samson factory was scrupulous about marking its nearly perfect copies so that they would not be confused with the originals, though these marks have sometimes been erased later by dishonest dealers and collectors. (A detail of the Samson mark on the elephant is illustrated on p. 193.)

Fig. 116
COVERED JAR
France, Samson & Cie., c. 1850–1900
H: 28.5 cm G05.11.08

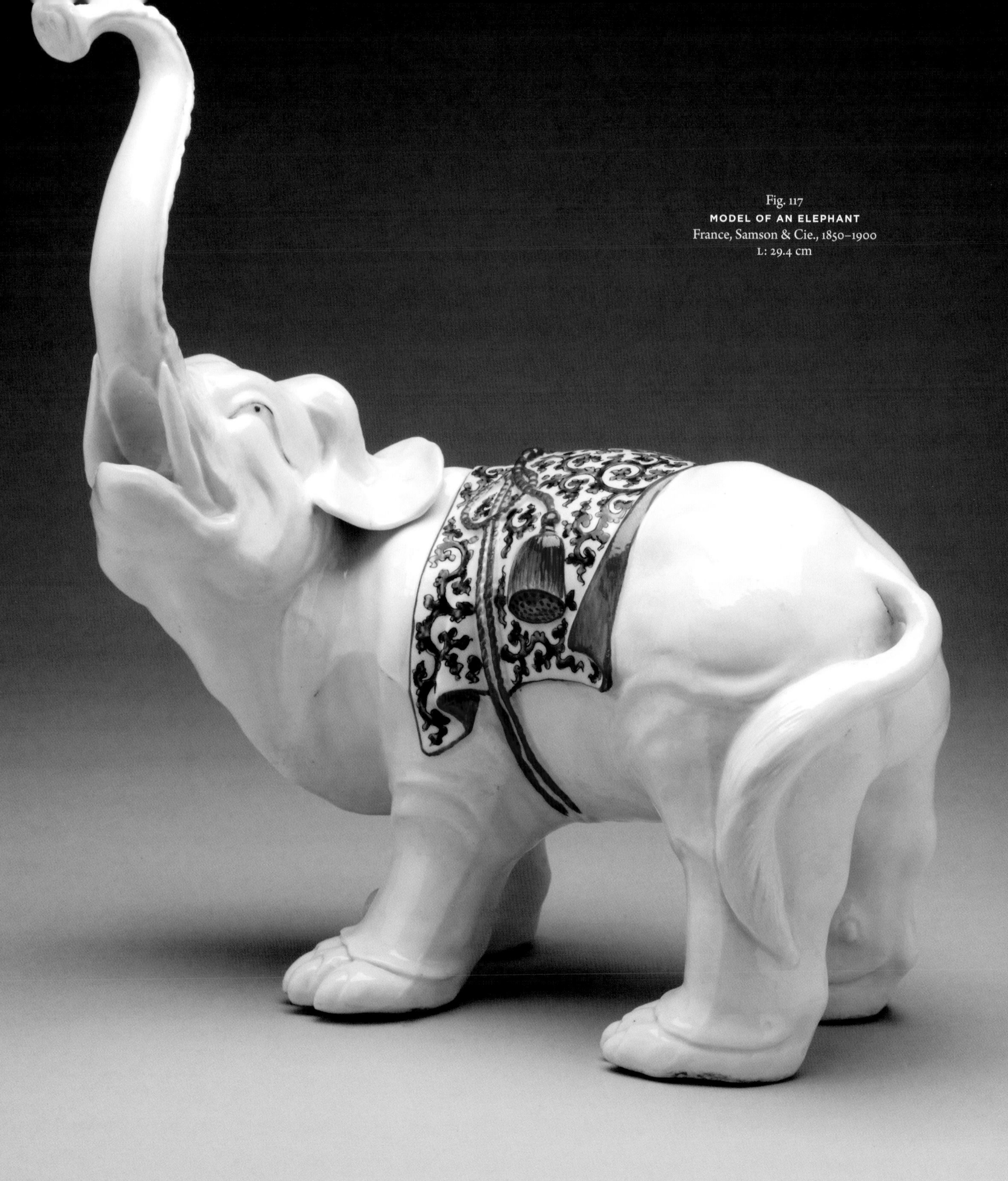

Fig. 117
MODEL OF AN ELEPHANT
France, Samson & Cie., 1850–1900
L: 29.4 cm

THE JAPANESE STYLE IN EUROPE: **ENGLAND**

Fig. 118
SAUCE BOAT WITH QUAIL DESIGN
Chinese porcelain, c. 1730–40
decorated in England, c. 1740–50
L: 23.5 cm

THE ENGLISH CERAMIC INDUSTRY developed later than its counterparts on the continent.[116] In the seventeenth century, English ceramics were dominated by tin-glazed earthenware very similar to the kind produced in the Netherlands. In the early eighteenth century, tin-glazed earthenware was gradually supplanted by more durable salt-glazed stoneware. The first porcelain was not produced in England until the mid-1740s. This porcelain, a variety of soft-paste porcelain, was produced by the Chelsea factory on the outskirts of London. Within a few years, several more English factories opened that also produced different varieties of soft-paste porcelain. Although some English potters experimented with true hard-paste porcelain production as early as the 1760s, it did not become a commercially viable product in England until the end of the eighteenth century. Unlike the porcelain factories on the continent that received funding from aristocratic patrons, the English porcelain factories were all commercial enterprises that succeeded or failed based on the competitive merits of their products. As a result, many factories operated for relatively short periods, and there were numerous bankruptcies and mergers.

Japanese porcelains first gained popularity among the English aristocracy during the 1670s and 80s. A famous 1688 inventory of the contents of Burghley House in Lincolnshire lists more than one hundred pieces of Japanese porcelain.[117] However, the appreciation of Japanese porcelain in England seems to have remained confined mainly to the nobility until the 1740s, when Japanese designs first began to appear on English ceramics made for the broader commercial market. Many English porcelain factories produced Japanese-inspired wares for the mass market in the 1750s and 60s, before interest in those designs gradually waned and was replaced by a demand for the French Rococo and, later, Neoclassical styles. Japanese designs were revived again in the 1820s and in the 1860s and 70s by several English factories seeking to capitalize once more on their exotic appeal and association with aristocratic tastes. (For example, see fig. 157.)

Salt-glazed stoneware was made by shovelling salt into the kiln at the height of the firing process.[118] The salt vaporized in the intense heat and reacted with chemicals in the clay to create a shiny glaze. Salt glazing was first developed in Germany during the fifteenth century and became popular in England during the first half of the eighteenth century. Although salt-glazed stonewares were not as white or as strong as porcelain, they were more durable than traditional lead- and tin-glazed earthenware and offered an attractive alternative to consumers who could not afford porcelain.

Most English salt-glazed stonewares were made in Staffordshire or in London and decorated with traditional English designs. A smaller number, however, were decorated with Chinese- and Japanese-influenced designs. The decoration on the two London pieces illustrated here is especially fine, and the form of the teapot with the crane design is also notably unusual.

Fig. 119
PLATE WITH CRANE DESIGN
England, London, c. 1745–55
D: 21.8 cm

Fig. 120
TEAPOT WITH CRANE DESIGN
England, London, c. 1745–55
L: 14.7 cm

Fig. 121
TEAPOT WITH FLORAL DESIGN
England, Staffordshire, c. 1745–55
L: 16 cm

Fig. 122
ACANTHUS-LEAF TEAPOT
England, Chelsea factory, c. 1745–49
L: 16 cm G05.11.10

The Chelsea factory was the first in England to produce porcelain.[119] Chelsea porcelain was a variety of soft-paste porcelain made from a mixture of clay and crushed glassy frit. It could be thrown on a wheel but was also well suited to shaping in a mould. The body of this early Chelsea teapot was moulded to resemble an acanthus leaf, a long-established motif in European art and architecture.[120] Somewhat incongruously, the teapot is also painted with a Japanese-influenced tiger and bamboo design.

Provenance (the history of ownership) is an important part of an object's historical and commercial value. Many objects in the Macdonald Collection formerly belonged to important Japanese and European private collections. This teapot, for example, once belonged to Mrs. Shand Kidd, the mother of Princess Diana.

Fig. 123
HEXAGONAL TEAPOT WITH LADY IN A PAVILION
England, Chelsea factory, c. 1750–52
L: 17.5 cm

Japanese porcelain was not commonly available in England when the Chelsea factory opened. But Chelsea decorators had access to some older aristocratic collections of Japanese porcelain through one of the factory's financial backers, Sir Everard Fawkener, private secretary to the Duke of Cumberland. They also had access to a collection of Japanese-style Meissen porcelains through Sir Charles Hanbury Williams, the former British envoy to the court of Saxony.[121] These models allowed the Chelsea factory to produce extremely accurate imitations of Japanese forms and designs, as can be seen on this hexagonal teapot decorated with a version of the aristocratic woman in a garden motif (see fig. 70).[122]

Fig. 124
PLATE WITH DRAGON AND TIGER DESIGN
England, Chelsea factory, c. 1750–52
W: 23 cm G04.18.21

The founder of the Chelsea factory, Nicholas Sprimont, began his career as a silversmith, and many early Chelsea porcelains—such as this plate—were inspired by silver forms.[123] This plate belongs to a well-known service made up of silver-inspired forms decorated with a traditional Japanese dragon and tiger motif.[124] The dish is a good example of the Rococo style that first gained popularity in France during the 1730s and soon spread to other countries in Europe. The Rococo style is characterized by asymmetrical, curvilinear forms inspired by shells, plants, vines and other elements from the natural world.

Fig. 125
PAIR OF SMALL HEXAGONAL JARS
England, Chelsea factory, c. 1752–55
H: 16.9 cm G05.12.6.1-2

In the late seventeenth century, England's Queen Mary II brought a small collection of Japanese porcelains from the Netherlands to her new Hampton Court palace. Among those porcelains was a pair of large Kakiemon-style hexagonal jars similar to the piece illustrated on the right. Those jars must at some point have been shown to the potters at the Chelsea factory, who produced a number of nearly identical copies.[125] They also created some smaller versions of the same basic form, such as the jars above.[126]

Fig. 126
LARGE HEXAGONAL COVERED JAR
England, Chelsea factory, c. 1752–55
H: 28.5 cm

Fig. 127
LEAF-FORM DISH WITH DRAGON AND TIGER DESIGN
England, Chelsea factory, c. 1752–55
W: 21.8 cm G04.18.20

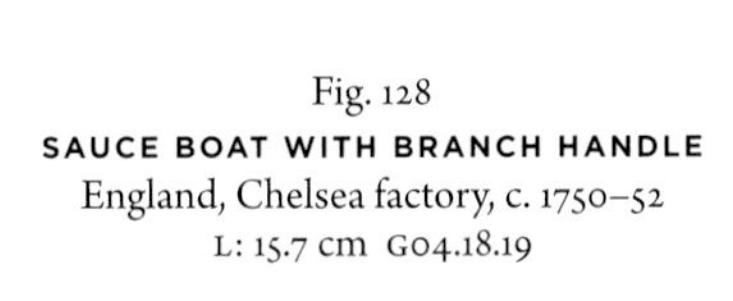

Fig. 128
SAUCE BOAT WITH BRANCH HANDLE
England, Chelsea factory, c. 1750–52
L: 15.7 cm G04.18.19

Fig. 129
CREAM PITCHER
England, Chelsea factory, c. 1752–55
L: 12.3 cm G04.19.23

Fig. 130
PLATE WITH AMOROUS COUPLE
England, Chelsea factory, c. 1755
W: 24.5 cm G05.11.12

Fig. 131
OCTAGONAL PLATE WITH PHOENIX AND PRUNUS
England, Chelsea factory, c. 1752–55
W: 25 cm

Fig. 132
TEAPOT WITH PEONY AND PRUNUS DESIGN
England, Chelsea factory, c. 1750–52
L: 17.5 cm G05.11.09

This teapot is decorated with four panels depicting peonies and prunus blossoms set against vividly coloured red and green backgrounds. The inspiration for this rare design may have come from the panels on some Kakiemon jars (see fig. 126, for example) or possibly from Japanese Imari ware.

Like many of the teapots illustrated in this book, this teapot is rather small in comparison to modern examples. Tea was very expensive in Europe during the seventeenth and eighteenth centuries, and people typically steeped enough for only one or two cups at a time.

Fig. 133
INKWELL
England, Bow factory, dated 1750
D: 8.9 cm G05.12.2

The Bow factory was established in 1747 (or possibly somewhat earlier) by a consortium of businessmen who wanted to claim a share of the Chinese porcelain trade.[127] Their aspirations were reflected in the name they chose for their factory, New Canton, after the Chinese port where the English trade in Asia was headquartered. This inkwell belongs to a well-known group of inkwells that are inscribed with the name of the Bow factory and the dates 1750 and 1751.[128] The inkwell combines a Japanese banded hedge design with a Chinese colour palette and may have been created to advertise the new factory's familiarity with the most popular types of Asian porcelain.

Fig. 134
PAIR OF GLOBULAR VASES
England, Bow factory, c. 1755
H: 20 cm G05.12.04.1-2

Fig. 135
TWO HEXAGONAL VASES
England, Bow factory, c. 1755
H: 24 cm and 23.5 cm G05.12.03.1-2

Fig. 136
TUREEN AND STAND
England, Bow factory, c. 1755
Tureen H: 22.2 cm
Stand D: 34.7 cm G07.18.03-04

After the Chelsea factory began to imitate French porcelains in the mid-1750s, the Bow factory became the leading producer of Japanese-style porcelains in England.[129] Bow decorators often combined Japanese and Chinese influences in their work. This tureen and stand, for example, mix Japanese crane and tortoise motifs with Chinese-style blossoming trees and border motifs.[130] The handles and moulded mask forms at the ends of the tureen are borrowed from Meissen prototypes. The decoration on Bow porcelains was often eclectic in this way.

Fig. 137
TEAPOT WITH QUAIL
England, Bow factory, c. 1755–60
L: 16.8 cm

Bow decorators were especially fond of the Japanese quail design and it became one of their most popular motifs.[131] In England, the quail design was often called the "partridge" design. Most English consumers were not familiar with the original Chinese and Japanese meanings of the quail motif but appreciated it because it was a familiar and commonly hunted game bird. The quails on Bow porcelains are often schematically drawn and unnaturally coloured, as one might expect if the decorators were copying a design rather than trying to depict actual birds.

LOBED TEAPOT WITH CRAB DESIGN
England, Worcester factory, c. 1754
L: 18.8 cm

In 1752, it absorbed the Lund factory in Bristol and quickly emerged as an important force in the field of English porcelain.[132] Worcester produced a distinctive type of porcelain made from China clay and soaprock (steatite) that was strong, brilliantly white and highly resistant to thermal shock. It was an immediate commercial success. The Worcester influenced designs from the early 1750s, as this teapot demonstrates. But Japanese designs did not become a major part of Worcester's repertoire until the late 1750s and 60s, after Chelsea and Bow had already created a market for those patterns.[133]

Fig. 139
BELL-SHAPED 1MUG
England, Worcester factory, c. 1752
H: 9.4 cm

The form of this mug is based on a silver or pewter prototype. Its design of flowers and butterflies is very sensitively painted, wrapping around the surface of the mug and creating an effective balance of positive and negative spaces. The combination of the form, design and bright enamels suggests that this mug dates to around the time the Worcester and Lund's Bristol factories merged.

Fig. 140
CREAM JUG WITH BIRD ON ROCK
England, Worcester factory, c. 1765–70
H: 13.3 cm

Fig. 141
LEAF-FORM DISH
England, Worcester factory, c. 1755–58
W: 21.4 cm G04.18.28

Fig. 142
BOWL WITH BANDED HEDGE DESIGN
England, Vauxhall factory, dated 1762
D: 14.3 cm

The Vauxhall China Works operated from 1751 to 1764.[134] It was a small factory that produced mainly blue and white porcelains and overglaze enamel-decorated porcelains in the Chinese style. Japanese-style designs were unusual at Vauxhall. The covered vase illustrated here combines a simplified Japanese banded hedge design with a French Rococo form. The bowl combines Japanese banded hedges with Chinese export-style flowering trees and border motifs. The base of the bowl is inscribed with the date 1762, making it a very rare documentary piece for the Vauxhall factory (see a detail of the mark on p. 193).

Fig. 143
COVERED VASE
England, Vauxhall factory, c. 1755–60
H: 14.6 cm

COMPARISONS

Fig. 144
OVOID FLASK
Japan, Arita, c. 1680–1700
H: 23.3 cm G07.18.10.1
OVOID FLASK
Germany, Meissen factory, c. 1730
H: 21 cm G05.11.5

top, Fig. 145
OCTAGONAL BOWL WITH SEASONAL FLOWERS
Japan, Arita, c. 1690–1710
W: 12 cm
OCTAGONAL BOWL WITH SEASONAL FLOWERS
England, Chelsea factory, c. 1752–55
W: 11.5 cm G04.18.24

bottom, Fig. 146
SCALLOPED DISH WITH PINE, PRUNUS AND BAMBOO
Japan, Arita, c. 1680–1700
W: 14.8 cm G05.12.19
SCALLOPED DISH WITH PINE, PRUNUS AND BAMBOO
England, Chelsea factory, c. 1752–55
W: 18 cm G05.12.05

top, Fig. 147
DISH WITH ROOSTER DESIGN
Japan, Arita, c. 1700–10
W: 22.5 cm G04.18.44

bottom, Fig. 148
DISH WITH ROOSTER DESIGN
China, Jingdezhen, c. 1710–20
W: 19 cm
DISH WITH ROOSTER DESIGN
England, Bow factory, c. 1755
W: 19.6 cm G04.18.26

top, Fig. 149
DECAGONAL PLATE WITH PHOENIX DESIGN
Japan, Arita, c. 1690–1700
W: 23.1 cm
OCTAGONAL PLATE WITH PHOENIX DESIGN
Germany, c. 1750
W: 23.8 cm G04.18.02

bottom, Fig. 150
PLATE WITH PHOENIX DESIGN
England, Chelsea factory, c. 1752–55
D: 23.5 cm

Fig. 151
OCTAGONAL PLATE WITH SHIBA ONKO DESIGN
Japan, Arita, c. 1680–1700
W: 21 cm
OCTAGONAL PLATE WITH SHIBA ONKO DESIGN
Austria, c. 1750
W: 18.8 cm

top, Fig. 152
SCALLOPED TEABOWL AND SAUCER WITH CHINESE BOYS DESIGN
Germany, Meissen factory, c. 1730
Bowl H: 6.6 cm; Saucer D: 15.5 cm

bottom, Fig. 153
SCALLOPED TEABOWL AND SAUCER WITH CHINESE BOYS DESIGN
France, Chantilly factory, c. 1730–40
Bowl H: 6.8 cm; Saucer D: 14.7 cm

top left, Fig. 154
PLATE WITH *KRAAK*-STYLE BIRD DESIGN
Japan, Arita, c. 1690
D: 20.5 cm

top right, Fig. 155
PLATE WITH *KRAAK*-STYLE BIRD DESIGN
Japan, Arita, c. 1690–1710
D: 21.9 cm

bottom, Fig. 156
PLATE WITH *KRAAK*-STYLE BIRD DESIGN
England, Chelsea factory, c. 1755
D: 23.3 cm

Fig. 157
TEAPOT, TEACUP, SAUCER AND BOWL WITH GRAPE AND SQUIRREL DESIGN
England, Spode factory, c. 1820
Teapot L: 24 cm
Cup H: 5.2 cm; Saucer D: 14.5 cm
Bowl D: 17.5 cm

Fig. 158
PAIR OF ELEPHANTS AND BUDDHIST FIGURE
France, Samson & Cie, c. 1850–1900
Elephants H: 25.1 cm
Buddhist Figure H: 22.9 cm

Detail of mark on fig. 23

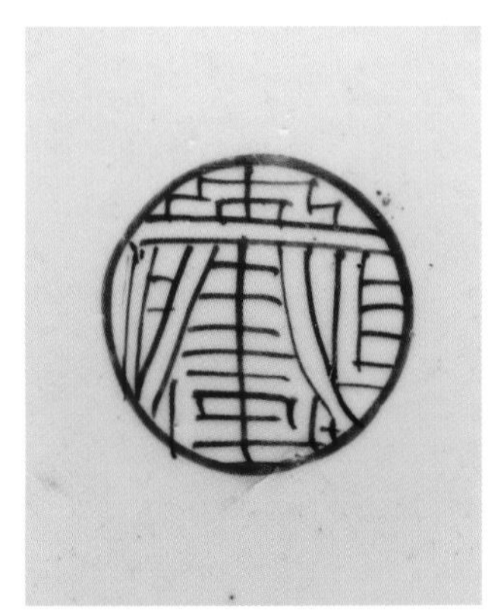

Detail of mark on fig. 39

Detail of mark on fig. 56

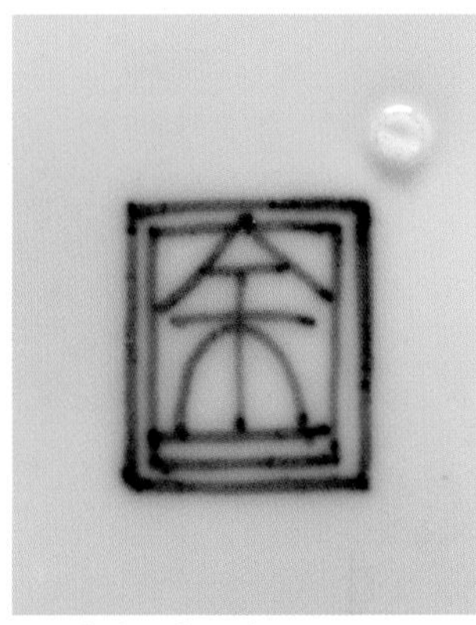

Detail of mark on fig. 81

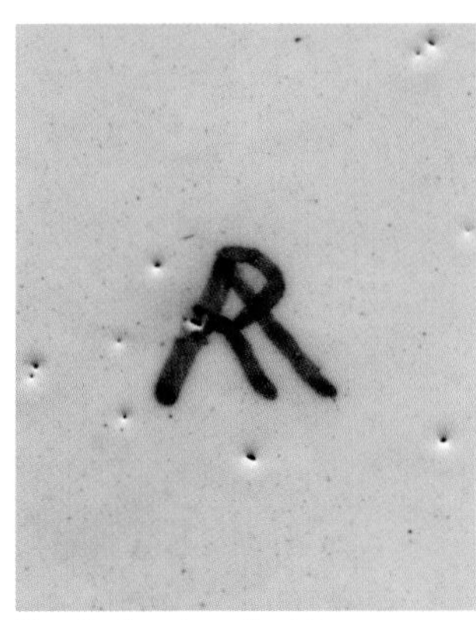

Detail of mark on fig. 86

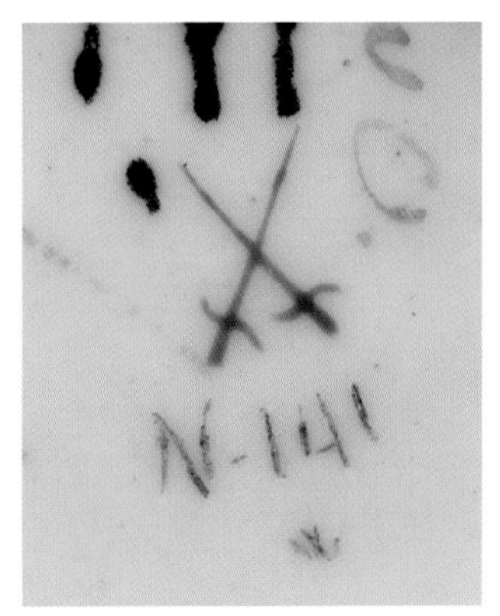

Detail of mark on fig. 96

Detail of mark on fig. 117

Detail of mark on fig. 142

NOTES

ADAPTATION AND INNOVATION: PORCELAIN IN JAPAN, 1600–1750
CHARLES MASON

1. Much of the information in this section is synthesized and summarized from longer discussions of Tokugawa-period history in Schirokauer 1993; Totman 1993; Jansen 2000.
2. Hayashiya and Trubner 1977.
3. Jansen 1992.
4. Takeuchi 2003; Varley and Kumakura 1989, chaps. 5 and 6.
5. Curtis 2006.
6. Murase 2003.
7. For a fuller discussion of the facts and myths related to the discovery of porcelain in Japan, see Jenyns 1965, chap. 3. Also Reichel 1981, pp. 36 and 54.
8. Impey 1996.
9. Records preserved by the Nabeshima clan that ruled Saga prefecture in the seventeenth century indicate that members of the Taku family acted as their agents in supervising the Arita porcelain industry. See Impey 2002a, p. 16.
10. Wilson 2001, p. 45.
11. The Karatsu stoneware industry played an important role in the formation of the Arita porcelain industry. See Seattle Art Museum 1972, pp. 30–31.
12. Impey 1996, p. 3.
13. Impey 1996.
14. Ohashi 1991.
15. The so-called alternate attendance regulations were issued in 1634, but it took some years before all of the provincial daimyo established residences in the capital. See Guth 1996, pp. 14–15.
16. Hanley 1997.
17. The decrease in Chinese porcelain imports caused such a demand gap that new porcelain factories were established in two other places besides Arita. These factories—at Kutani in Kaga prefecture and Himetani in Bingo prefecture—were small, relatively short-lived and did not have much impact beyond their local areas. But the fact that they were founded at all is significant evidence of porcelain's growing popularity in the 1650s. See Idemitsu Museum 2004, pp. 26 and 227.
18. Jörg 2003.
19. Impey 1990b.
20. Nagatake 2003, pp. 54–56.
21. Idemitsu Museum 2004.
22. Nagatake 2003.
23. Rotondo-McCord and Bufton 1997. Also Nagatake 2003.
24. Kyushu Ceramic Museum 2006.
25. Singer 1997; Lawrence 1997.
26. Vaporis 1998, p. 83.
27. For examples, see Swinton 1995, p. 141 and plates 2, 3, 4, 6 and 7; T. Clark 1992, pp. 88–89.
28. Totman 1993.
29. For a discussion of the so-called Chinese Imari phenomenon, see Ayers, Impey and Mallet 1990, pp. 233–38.
30. Impey 2002a, p. 28.

THE ORIGINS AND EVOLUTION OF KAKIEMON
OLIVER IMPEY

1. The Japanese literature on Kakiemon is, of course, extensive; for the best recent discussion, see Kyushu Ceramic Museum 1999 (hereafter KCM 1999). Jenyns 1965 is the most extensive discussion in English but is now largely superseded; for recent discussions in English, see Hinton and Impey 1989; Impey 2002a. English-language references will be cited as far as possible; for Japanese bibliographies, see Nishida 1974; KCM 1999; Impey 2002a.
2. See Arita Board of Education 1978, 1979.
3. For a discussion of this, see Impey 1997. There are, for instance, some blue and white dishes strikingly similar to some found at Chokichidani, a kiln that ceased production at about the time that Nangawara B was established. Possibly the workshop simply transferred its patronage to the new kiln.
4. Nishida 1974, chap. 1.
5. Volker 1959; Viallé 2000a.
6. Impey 1973.
7. Nagatake 1974.
8. For the classic account, see Okochi 1916. For a good discussion in English, see Nishida 1974.
9. Nagatake 1974.
10. Sato 1973. The fact that Kyoto enamels are on a low-fired body is irrelevant.
11. Impey 1984.
12. Jenyns 1965.
13. Nishida 1974.
14. Translation by Nishida 1974.
15. The present author has not seen the documents, nor could he comment on them if he had. Belief rests entirely upon the content as translated by Nishida 1974. Nishida rejects the authenticity for reasons with which the present author disagrees, notably her conflation of the continuation of trade in Imari wares with a supposed continuation of trade in Kakiemon wares.
16. KCM 1999. I am grateful to Menno Fitski for his assistance with this section. See also Fitski 2002.
17. KCM 1999, nos. 236 (bowl) and 237 (mould).
18. See Arita Board of Education 1978, 1979 and 1992; Impey 2002a.
19. Impey 1990a; KCM 1999.
20. Moulds for figures found at the site included two well-known Imari types, the standing male figure and the roistering Dutchman sitting on a barrel. There were at least two types of standing *bijin* figures, as well as tortoises, ducks and parrots all intended for Kakiemon enamels, as well as some other figures; Impey 1990a; KCM 1999. An example of the tall *bijin* (see fig. 60) is illustrated in a book of 1807, where it is stated that it was made by Kakiemon; Kawazu 1807; KCM 1999, p. 42. This is important as an early recognition of Kakiemon products.
21. Sakaida Kakiemon XIII, personal communication, 1971.
22. Volker 1954; Volker 1959; Jörg 2003.
23. The shipping lists, that is, the actual bills of lading, from 1650 to 1660, transcribed and translated by Menno Fitski, are printed in Impey 1996, chap. 12.
24. Impey 1996, p. 135.
25. Volker 1954, pp. 136–37 quotes Zacharias Wagenaer's famous letter of 1659 claiming the invention of a pattern using gold and silver on a blue ground.
26. Volker 1954, p. 152; Lang 1983; Impey 2002a, fig. 1. The tortoise is not listed in the 1688 inventory.
27. For definitions of Early Enamelled Ware, see Ayers, Impey and Mallet 1990; Impey 2002a.
28. Impey 1973.
29. Lang 1983. For Japanese porcelain in the Burghley House inventory, see Impey 2002b.
30. See Ayers, Impey and Mallet 1990, nos. 148–49.
31. Arita Board of Education 1992; Impey 2002a, pp. 118–19.
32. Impey 1990b, p. 20.
33. Boltz 1980; Cassidy-Geiger 1994.
34. Kyushu Ceramic Museum 1984.
35. KCM 1999, pp. 121–38. Some, indeed, imitate Nabeshima (KCM 1999, nos. 233, 262), an interesting parallel to the imitation of Kakiemon by the Imaemon family in the early twentieth century (Impey 2002a, no. 414).
36. See Ayers, Impey and Mallet 1990.

"THE COLOURS OF OLD JAPAN": JAPANESE EXPORT PORCELAIN, KAKIEMON AND EUROPEAN IMITATIONS
CHRISTIAAN J.A. JÖRG

1. There are many publications dealing with the cultural and commercial interaction between Japan and the Netherlands, but mostly they focus on specific aspects. The best general survey in English is still Boxer 1950.
2. Again, there is a wide range of publications available. The first modern, comprehensive study is Jenyns 1965. Impey 2002a and Jörg 2003 are the most recent surveys and include extensive bibliographies on the subject.
3. The basic works are Volker 1954 and Volker 1959. For an indispensable addition, based on the actual shipping lists, see Viallé 2000a, pp. 176–83; Viallé 2000b, pp. 197–205.
4. Thus far, the only monograph in a Western language on Shoki-Imari and the archaeology of the early kilns is Impey 1996.
5. The subject has not yet been studied in depth. For some scattered bits of information, see Jörg 2001.
6. See Volker 1954, pp. 34–112. For additional historical context, see Jörg 1993, pp. 183–94.

7. The standard work on *kraak* porcelain is Rinaldi 1989.
8. For the most recent publication on this subject, see Curtis 2006.
9. The classic work on transitional porcelain is Kilburn 1981. See also Little 1983; Curtis 1995; Butler, Curtis and Little 2002.
10. This coexistence became evident from the salvaged porcelain cargo of the so-called Hatcher wreck, datable to c. 1643, in which *kraak* and transitional porcelains were mixed; see Kilburn 1988.
11. Impey 1996, pp. 99–124. See ibid., p. 59, fig. 48 for a cluster of stoneware and porcelain fragments fused together in the Mukaenohara kiln, proving that both types were fired at the same time, maybe during an experimental phase.
12. The most recent general survey of Dutch Delftware in English is van Dam 2004. See also Fourest 1980. For the influence of Oriental ceramics on Dutch Delftware, see Jörg 1984.
13. Impey 1996, pp. 132–34, gives the shipments in the 1650s and their prices. Viallé 2000a deals with shipments only for Holland, not with those for Batavia and the inter-Asian trade as Impey does.
14. For details on these and following orders and the subsequent shipments, see Viallé 2000a, pp. 176–77.
15. Several "Wagenaer" pieces are still extant in public collections, identified by their overall dark underglaze blue and a faded flower scroll or fishnet decoration in silver or gold. See Impey 2002a, cat. no. 10; Jörg 2003, cat. nos. 173, 174; Ayers, Impey and Mallet 1990, cat. no. 35. It is not certain if these pieces were indeed part of the shipment of 1659, because almost immediately the Japanese potters made copies that were offered in porcelain shops in Nagasaki, much to the annoyance of Wagenaer; see Volker 1954, pp. 136–37. Company employees therefore could have bought similar "modern" wares privately.
16. Impey 1996, pp. 132–39.
17. Viallé 2000b, pp. 197–98.
18. For examples of these wares, see Impey 2002a, cat. nos. 57, 58, 64–68; Jörg 2003, cat. nos. 34–36, 49, 50. The celadons from the Maruo and Hasami kilns were used for export too, as were the early Kutani-style wares.
19. Jörg 1992.
20. Impey 1996, pp. 99–116.
21. Japan Society 1986, cat. nos. 18–34.
22. Ströber 2001, figs. 55–65.
23. Spriggs 1967, pp. 73–87, plates 79b, c.
24. Jörg 2003, p. 38, fig. 21a.
25. For this technique the porcelain painter used real ink. When fired, the ink burned away, leaving lighter lines in the underglaze blue. I would like to thank Menno Fitski, Curator of the Japanese Art Department at the Rijksmuseum Amsterdam, for providing this information.
26. For dishes of this type, see Jörg 2003, cat. nos. 21, 22; Japan Society 1986, cat. no. 19.
27. Impey 1990c, p. 27; see also Impey 2002a, pp. 21–24.
28. Impey 2005, p. 4.
29. There was a substantial trade in Chinese porcelain to Japan by the Portuguese, the Dutch, the Japanese and the Chinese, but as far as I know no specific references are made to the wares now called "Swatow," nor is it known if the often-mentioned "coarse porcelains" in VOC records were Swatow. For this trade in general, see Impey and Tregear 1983; Jörg 1993. For Swatow in a modern Japanese collection, see Seikado Bunko Art Museum 1997; for eighteenth- and nineteenth-century Japanese imitations of Swatow wares, proving they had remained popular in Japan, see Aichi Prefectural Ceramic Museum 1980.
30. Impey 1990b, pp. 21–22.
31. Godden 1979, pp. 301–31.
32. The discussion was started by Oliver Impey when he suggested that Kakiemon might have appealed to the Chinese: see Impey 1990b, p. 20. However, the former imperial collections in Beijing include all sorts of export wares, even *chine de commande,* but as far as I know, no Kakiemon. If the Chinese bought it themselves, examples would likely have been found in China, but there seem to be none. Therefore Impey's suggestion needs further proof.
33. I would like to define the term *Kakiemon* rather loosely and include pieces painted in Kakiemon-style produced by Arita competitors, showing the same restrained, elegant and soft-coloured decorations.
34. Impey 2002a, p. 26.
35. I would like to thank Charles Mason of the Gardiner Museum, Toronto, for initiating a discussion about these and other points. Indications of domestic interest in Kakiemon are scattered, but do exist: for instance shards found at daimyo residences, or the illustration of a Kakiemon *bijin* in a Japanese essay for antique collectors of 1807. See Fitski 2002, p. 29, notes 49 and 50.
36. For surveys of Imari wares, see the sections in Impey 2002a; Jörg 2003; and the bibliographic references there.
37. An excellent example of such a Chinese porcelain shipment is the so-called Vung Tau cargo, salvaged from a Chinese junk that shipwrecked in the 1690s on its way to Batavia; see Jörg and Flecker 2001.
38. For this section on Dutch Delftware I relied on Jörg 1984; van Dam 2004; and the literature mentioned there.
39. Godden 1979, p. 339.
40. Jörg 2001, p. 63.
41. For a recent survey of overdecorated Delft, including porcelain overdecorated in Germany and England, see Espir 2005. For Kakiemon imitations in Amsterdams Bont, see ibid., pp. 78–91. See also Godden 1979, pp. 363–75.
42. For this section on European imitations I have heavily leaned on the contributions of J.V.G. Mallet and Anthony du Boulay in Ayers, Impey and Mallet 1990. In addition, I have consulted general surveys such as Weiss 1971; Godden 1979, pp. 339–62; Musée Cernuschi 2007, which has a large section on European ceramics with chinoiserie designs. For the generally known facts on the European factories I do not give bibliographical references.
43. For an up-to-date survey of Meissen porcelain and its cultural context, see Cassidy-Geiger 2008.
44. Kakiemon-style decorations may occasionally have appeared on Meissen in the mid-1720s, though there is confusion about dates. In Musée Cernuschi 2007, earlier dates for Kakiemon-style Meissen are given than is usually done; see ibid., cat. nos. 67, 68 and 75.
45. For a survey of Oriental, in particular Kakiemon, designs on Meissen porcelain, see Shono 1973.
46. Mallet 1990, pp. 45–47.
47. Nelson and Impey 1994.
48. Mallet 1990, p. 53.
49. du Boulay 1990, p. 277.
50. Worcester pieces with a monochrome ground and reserved panels are usually associated with Meissen models; however, I would suggest here that Kangxi powder-blue pieces, widely available in England, might have been a more likely source of inspiration.
51. Mallet 1990, p. 55.
52. Le Corbeiller 1992.

HIGHLIGHTS OF THE MACDONALD COLLECTION

CHARLES MASON

1. Ayers 1988.
2. Impey 2002a, pp. 19–20.
3. Murase 2003, p. 120; National Museum of Japanese History 1998. A late sixteenth-century screen painting that depicts this way of eating is illustrated in Cunningham 1991, pp. 94–95.
4. Several complete sets of dishes are illustrated in Kyushu Ceramic Museum 1991, pp. 44–45.
5. Seventeenth-century Japanese silk dyeing techniques are discussed at length in Gluckman 1992.
6. Fragments of similar dishes have been discovered at the Yamagoya kiln site in Arita. Other intact dishes that use this combination of underglaze blue and iron-brown glaze are illustrated in Ayers, Impey and Mallet 1990, p. 89; C. Shimizu 2002, p. 39.
7. The Chinese origins of this technique are discussed in Little 1983, p. 46; Curtis 2006, p. 114.
8. A very similar dish, possibly from the same workshop, exists in the Shibata Collection at the Kyushu Ceramic Museum. See Kyushu Ceramic Museum 1991, p. 9.
9. Another dish with a similar image of an egret depicted in reserve on a blue ground is illustrated in Kyushu Ceramic Museum 1993, p. 28.
10. A complete set of square ship bottles is illustrated in Ayers, Impey and Mallet 1990, p. 108.
11. Kyushu Ceramic Museum 1998, pp. 24–47.
12. For example, see Kyushu Ceramic Museum 1991, pp. 32–33.
13. Kyushu Ceramic Museum 1996, p. 31.
14. A screen painting by Kano Tanyu (1602–1674) with an image of tigers and bamboo is illustrated in Y. Shimizu 1988, pp. 203–204 and 206.
15. The spade-shaped motif on the border of the egret dish derives from Chinese art and represents

a magical fungus that supposedly confers good luck and long life.
16. Curtis 2006, p. 33.
17. A late seventeenth-century *kosode* gown with an abstract roundel pattern is illustrated in Gluckman 1992, p. 243. For another porcelain dish with a similar design, see Kyushu Ceramic Museum 1990, p. 10.
18. Jörg 2003, pp. 38–39.
19. For example, see Kyushu Ceramic Museum 1991, p. 73.
20. Barry Davies 1997, p. 108.
21. Trubner 1988.
22. Kyoto National Museum 2006, pp. 59–93; Y. Shimizu 1988, pp. 318–321.
23. Impey 2002a, pp. 21–24.
24. Ayers, Impey and Mallet 1990, p. 177.
25. Morita 2007.
26. The enamels used on this bowl recall Chinese Swatow wares. See Harrison 1979; Seattle Art Museum 1988, pp. 38–40 and 159.
27. Impey 2002a, p. 50.
28. Dishes similar to the larger example shown here are illustrated in Kyushu Ceramic Museum 1990, p. 184; Ayers, Impey and Mallet 1990, p. 123.
29. Two related jars in the Ashmolean Museum are illustrated in Impey 2002a, p. 67.
30. A similar jar lacking its lid in the collection of the Ashmolean Museum is illustrated in Impey 2002a, p. 75.
31. Akiyama 1990, pp. 123–126; Guth 1996, pp. 55–56.
32. Similar jars are illustrated in Kyushu Ceramic Museum 1997, p. 36; C. Shimizu 2002, p. 87; Nagatake 2003, p. 29.
33. For example, see a screen with a scene from *The Tale of Genji* illustrated in Clark Center 2002, pp. 70–71 and 190. The Tosa school is briefly described in Guth 1996, pp. 57–59.
34. For example, two similar jars without lids are illustrated in Hinton and Impey 1989, p. 58. Also Christie's New York, 15 September 1999, lots 11 and 12.
35. The problems of the traditional nomenclature used to describe Japanese porcelains are discussed further in Impey 2002a, pp. 21–22.
36. Idemitsu Museum 2004; Y. Shimizu 1988, pp. 323–325.
37. Kyushu Ceramic Museum 1998, p. 172.
38. Ibid., pp. 174–75.
39. Mason 1993, p. 286.
40. Waste jars of this size were used for collecting the dregs and other waste water associated with tea preparation and drinking. Harrison-Hall 2001, p. 375.
41. A Chinese piece of different form but with related decoration is illustrated in Seattle Art Museum 1988, p. 118.
42. For example, see Little 1983, p. 85.
43. A pair of similar gourd-shaped flasks with longer necks is illustrated in Seattle Art Museum 1972, p. 143.
44. C. Shimizu 2002, p. 59. Also Kyushu Ceramic Museum 1998, pp. 186–89.
45. Seattle Art Museum 1972, p. 35.
46. Kyushu Ceramic Museum 2006; Y. Shimizu 1988, pp. 321–22.
47. Vaporis 1998, p. 87.
48. Kyushu Ceramic Museum 1996, p. 50.
49. Jenkins 1993, p. 214.
50. Other related pieces are illustrated in Ayers, Impey and Mallet 1990, p. 143; Nagatake 2003, p. 43; Jörg 2003, p. 102.
51. This style is discussed in Curtis 2006, pp. 70–71.
52. A similar Japanese dish in the Shibata Collection is illustrated in Kyushu Ceramic Museum 1991, fig. 441.
53. Kyushu Ceramic Museum 1996, p. 81; Idemitsu Museum 1984, p. 46.
54. The first figures exported to Europe in 1659 included several human-form figures and several figures of cranes. There is no indication that these figures were made specifically for export. Rather, they seem to have been pieces made for the Japanese domestic market that caught the fancy of a Dutch merchant. See Ayers, Impey and Mallet 1990, p. 175.
55. Discussions of Japanese porcelain figures almost always say that they were made exclusively for export. Yet archaeological evidence shows that ceramic sculptures were widely used within Japan during the seventeenth and eighteenth centuries. See Vaporis 1998, p. 88. There is also pictorial evidence for the manufacture and sale of ceramic figures to Japanese consumers. For example, see a 1770 woodblock print by Tachibana Minko depicting a potter making human and animal figures, illustrated in Baten 1995, p. 36.
56. A 1799 New Year's print by Akizuki Torin that depicts a courtesan with what appears to be an animal sculpture beside her is illustrated in McKee 2006, p. 47. The use of dolls and sculptures in festival parades is also discussed in McKee 2006, pp. 102–103.
57. This argument is discussed at greater length in Impey 2002a, p. 27.
58. Meech 1999, p. 11.
59. National Museum of Japanese History 1998. Numerous woodblock prints from the eighteenth and nineteenth centuries depict meals served on large dishes. For example, see Jenkins 1993, p. 112; Guth 1996, p. 123.
60. A similar food box tray in the Ashmolean Museum collection is discussed in Impey 2002a, p. 89.
61. Yamato-e was a painting style that evolved at the Heian court to depict native Japanese, rather than Chinese-inspired, subjects. See Mason 1993, pp. 126–27.
62. Kettles with this particular form of bail handle seem to be quite rare. Other examples of porcelain kettles are illustrated in Kyushu Ceramic Museum 1991, pp. 216–17. For a lacquer prototype, see Cunningham 1991, p. 122.
63. Ayers, Impey and Mallet 1990, pp. 175–89. Also Sargent 1991, pp. 249–252.
64. Similar figures are illustrated in Ayers, Impey and Mallet 1990, p. 180; Impey 2002a, p. 81; C. Shimizu 2002, p. 98. A painting of a similar subject is discussed in Murase 2003, pp. 214–15.
65. Similar figures are illustrated in Sargent 1991, p. 248; Kyushu Ceramic Museum 1996, p. 65; Nagatake 2003, pp. 27 and 47. Paintings of *bijin* are discussed in McKee 2006, pp. 122–123; Murase 2003, p. 270.
66. This dish, formerly in the collection of Richard de la Mare, was pictured on the cover of Soame Jenyn's groundbreaking 1965 book on Japanese porcelain.
67. The Sotatsu screen painting is in the collection of the Freer Gallery of Art in Washington, D.C.
68. Impey 2002a, p. 145.
69. Quail symbolism in Chinese ceramics is discussed in Butler, Curtis and Little 2002, p. 95; Curtis 2006, pp. 44–45.
70. Ayers, Impey and Mallet 1990, pp. 296–97; Cunningham 1991, pp. 36–37.
71. A set of five similar dishes is illustrated in Idemitsu Museum 1984, p. 26.
72. Other examples of these dishes are illustrated in Impey 2002a, pp. 132 and 159.
73. Ayers, Impey and Mallet 1990, p. 281.
74. Curtis 2006, p. 18.
75. Sima Guang was an important figure in the school of Neo-Confucian philosophy that was advocated by the Tokugawa government. See Schirokauer 1993, pp. 162–166. The popularity of this story with Japanese audiences is indicated by the existence of an early eighteenth-century woodcut illustrated in Keyes 1984, p. 246.
76. See Impey 2002a, p. 157; Idemitsu Museum 1984, p. 30.
77. For example, see Murase 2003, pp. 282–83; Ushioda 1992, pp. 70–71.
78. Other examples are illustrated in Ayers, Impey and Mallet 1990, p. 155; Impey 2002a, p. 164.
79. Banded hedges also appear in paintings of the period. For example, see a screen painting illustrated in Cunningham 1991, p. 84.
80. Earle 2000; Toshiro 1998.
81. For examples, see Ayers, Impey and Mallet 1990, pp. 120–21.
82. Varley and Kumakura 1989, pp. 182–184; Guth 1996, p. 38.
83. Den Blaauwen 2000, p. 216.
84. An ewer of similar form but with different decoration is illustrated in Ayers, Impey and Mallet 1990, p. 141.
85. A similar bowl is illustrated in Hinton and Impey 1989, p. 61.
86. Jörg 1982.
87. De Jonge 1969, pp. 14–20; Lange 2001, pp. 11–16.
88. Caiger-Smith 1973.
89. De Jonge 1969, p. 74.
90. A nearly identical dish is illustrated in Lunsingh Scheurleer 1984, p. 302.
91. De Jonge 1969, pp. 109–12 and pp. 116–19.
92. A nearly identical dish is illustrated in De Jonge 1965, p. 313.
93. Espir 2005; Lunsingh Scheurleer 1974, pp. 176–186.
94. The mark reads "N=79/".
95. Pietsch 1993, p. 7.
96. Reichel 1981, pp. 119–25.
97. Pietsch 1993, pp. 11–14; Mallet 1990, pp. 44–48.
98. A comparably early teapot decorated in the Kakiemon style is illustrated in Cummer Gallery of Art 1984, p. 193.
99. Other nearly identical copies of this flask are

illustrated in Cummer Gallery of Art 1984, p. 196; Den Blaauwen 2000, p. 225.
100. The Saxon royal collection inventory numbers are discussed in Reichel 1981, pp. 119–20. The mark on this flask reads "N=141/w".
101. Boltz 1980; Mallet 1990, pp. 44–45.
102. The ewer can be dated accurately by the silver mounts, which are hallmarked for Paris, 1731. The bottom of the ewer also has several fingernail marks deliberately impressed into the clay by the potter as an additional fraud detection device.
103. Another teabowl and saucer set with this design is illustrated in Cummer Gallery of Art 1984, p. 195.
104. A nearly identical teabowl and saucer set is illustrated in Pietsch 1993, pp. 90–91.
105. Tsang 1996.
106. A pair of Kakiemon beakers with the squirrel and grape design is illustrated in Nagatake 2003, p. 47.
107. Pietsch 1993, pp. 90–91.
108. Sotheby's New York, 26 September 1989, lot 11.
109. Rondot 1999; Lahaussois 1997.
110. LeDuc 1996; Roth and Le Corbeiller 2000, pp. 34–50.
111. LeDuc 1996, pp. 81–89.
112. Another Chantilly snuff box is discussed in Dawson 1996, p. 41.
113. LeDuc 1996, p. 399.
114. Dawson 1996, p. 20; LeDuc 1996, p. 365.
115. Dawson 1994, pp. 48–49.
116. G. Clark 1995; Lippert 1987.
117. Lang 1983; Impey 2002b.
118. G. Clark 1995, pp. 33–35.
119. Adams 2001; Lippert 1987, pp. 57–87.
120. The design is also called "Strawberry Leaf" in Chelsea pattern books. Additional examples are illustrated in Adams 2001, pp. 28–29.
121. Mallet 1990, p. 53.
122. Another example is illustrated in Adams 2001, p. 83.
123. Adams 2001, pp. 16–23.
124. See Idemitsu Museum 1984, no. 104; Ayers, Impey and Mallet 1990, p. 282.
125. See Ayers, Impey and Mallet 1990, pp. 172–173 and 201.
126. See Ayers, Impey and Mallet 1990, p. 202.
127. Adams and Redstone 1981; Lippert 1987, pp. 88–112.
128. Other examples are listed in Gabszewicz and Freeman 1982, pp. 19 and 52.
129. Gabszewicz and Freeman 1982, p. 42.
130. Several related pieces are illustrated and discussed in Begg and Taylor 2000, pp. 36–39.
131. Lippert 1987, pp. 93–95.
132. Spero 1984; Spero and Sandon 1996.
133. Spero 2005, pp. 215–227.
134. Cushion and Cushion 1992, pp. 100–105.

BIBLIOGRAPHY

Adams 2001
Adams, Elizabeth. *Chelsea Porcelain.* London: British Museum, 2001.

Adams and Redstone 1981
Adams, Elizabeth, and David Redstone. *Bow Porcelain.* London: Faber and Faber, 1981.

Aichi Prefectural Ceramic Museum 1980
Aichi Prefectural Ceramic Museum. *Inuyama-yaki ten* (Exhibition of Inuyama Wares). Nagoya: Aichi Prefectural Ceramic Museum, 1980.

Akiyama 1990
Akiyama, Terukazu. *Japanese Painting.* New York: Rizzoli, 1990.

Arita Board of Education 1978
Arita Board of Education, ed. *Preliminary Excavation of the Kakiemon Kiln Site, Arita.* Arita, 1978.

Arita Board of Education 1979
——. *Second Report on the Excavation of the Kakiemon Kiln Site, Arita.* Arita, 1979.

Arita Board of Education 1992
——. *Kusunokidani, Tenjinmachi, Hokaoyama: Report of the Precise Location of the Inner Town Group Kiln Sites, Arita.* Arita, 1992.

Ayers 1988
Ayers, John. "Blue-and-White and the Origins of Ming Porcelain Style." In Seattle Art Museum 1988, pp. 13–28.

Ayers, Impey and Mallet 1990
Ayers, John, Oliver Impey and J.V.G. Mallet. *Porcelain for Palaces: The Fashion for Japan in Europe, 1650–1750.* London: British Museum / Oriental Ceramic Society, 1990.

Barry Davies 1997
Barry Davies Oriental Art. *Ko-Imari Porcelain from the Collection of Oliver Impey.* London, 1997.

Baten 1995
Baten, Lea. *Playthings and Pastimes in Japanese Prints.* New York: Weatherhill, 1995.

Begg and Taylor 2000
Begg, Patricia, and Barry Taylor. *A Treasury of Bow.* Victoria: The Ceramics and Glass Circle of Australia, 2000.

Boltz 1980
Boltz, Claus. "Hoym, Lemaire und Meissen: Ein Beitrag zur Geschichte des Dresdener Porzellansammlung." *Keramos* 88 (1980).

Boxer 1950
Boxer, Charles R. *Jan Compagnie in Japan, 1600–1850.* 2nd rev. ed. The Hague: Martinus Nijhoff, 1950 (1st ed., 1936).

Butler, Curtis and Little 2002
Butler, Michael, Julia Curtis and Stephen Little. *Treasures from an Unknown Reign: Shunzhi Porcelain, 1644–1661.* Alexandria, Virginia: Art Services International, 2002.

Butler, Medley and Little 1990
Butler, Michael, Margaret Medley and Stephen Little. *Seventeenth-Century Chinese Porcelain from the Butler Family Collection.* Alexandria, Virginia: Art Services International, 1990.

Caiger-Smith 1973
Caiger-Smith, Alan. *Tin-Glaze Pottery in Europe and the Islamic World: The Tradition of 1000 Years in Maiolica, Faience and Delftware.* London: Faber and Faber, 1973.

Carpenter 2002
Carpenter, John T. *Kazari: Decoration and Display in Japan, 15th–19th Centuries.* London: British Museum, 2002.

Cassidy-Geiger 1994
Cassidy-Geiger, Maureen. "Returning to 'Hoym, Lemaire und Meissen.'" *Keramos* 146 (1994).

Cassidy-Geiger 2008
——. *The Arnhold Collection of Meissen Porcelain, 1710–1750.* New York: Frick Collection; London: D. Giles, 2008.

Christie's 1999
Christie's. *An Important Collection of Japanese Porcelain: Japanese and Korean Art.* New York: Christie's, 15 September 1999.

Clark Center 2002
Clark Center. *Delightful Pursuits: Highlights from the Lee Institute for Japanese Art at the Clark Center.* Japan: Nihon Keizai Shimbun, 2002.

G. Clark 1995
Clark, Garth. *The Potter's Art: A Complete History of Pottery in Britain.* London: Phaidon, 1995.

T. Clark 1992
Clark, Timothy. *Ukiyo-e Paintings in the British Museum.* London: British Museum, 1992.

Cummer Gallery of Art 1984
Cummer Gallery of Art. *The Wark Collection: Early Meissen Porcelain.* Jacksonville: Cummer Gallery of Art, 1984.

Cunningham 1991
Cunningham, Michael. *The Triumph of Japanese Style: 16th-Century Art in Japan.* Cleveland: Cleveland Museum of Art, 1991.

Curtis 1995
Curtis, Julia B. *Chinese Porcelains of the Seventeenth Century: Landscapes, Scholars' Motifs and Narratives.* New York: China Institute Gallery, 1995.

Curtis 2006
——. *Trade Taste and Transformation: Jingdezhen Porcelain for Japan, 1620–1645*. New York: China Institute Gallery, 2006.

Cushion and Cushion 1992
Cushion, John, and Margaret Cushion. *A Collector's History of British Porcelain*. Suffolk: Antique Collector's Club, 1992.

Dawson 1994
Dawson, Aileen. *A Catalogue of French Porcelain in the British Museum*. London: British Museum, 1994.

Dawson 1996
——. *Eighteenth-Century French Porcelain in the Ashmolean Museum*. Oxford: Ashmolean Museum, 1996.

De Jonge 1965
De Jonge, C.H. *Delfts Aardewerk v. 5*. Rotterdam: Nijgh & van Ditmar, 1965.

De Jonge 1969
——. *Delft Ceramics*. New York: Praeger, 1969.

Den Blaauwen 2000
Den Blaauwen, Abraham L. *Meissen Porcelain in the Rijksmuseum*. Amsterdam: Waanders, 2000.

du Boulay 1990
du Boulay, Anthony. "English Porcelain." In Ayers, Impey and Mallet 1990.

Earle 2000
Earle, Joe. *Infinite Spaces: The Art and Wisdom of the Japanese Garden*. Rutledge, Vermont: Charles E. Tuttle, 2000.

Espir 2005
Espir, Helen. *European Decoration on Oriental Porcelain, 1700–1830*. London: Jorge Welsh Books, 2005.

Fitski 2002
Fitski, Menno. *De haas en de maan: Arita-porselein in Japan, 1620–1820*. Amsterdam: Rijksmuseum, 2002.

Fourest 1980
Fourest, H.P. *Delftware: Faience Production at Delft*. New York: Rizzoli, 1980.

Gabszewicz 2000
Gabszewicz, Anton. *Made at New Canton: Bow Porcelain from the Collection of the London Borough of Newham*. London: English Ceramic Circle, 2000.

Gabszewicz and Freeman 1982
Gabszewicz, Anton, and Geoffrey Freeman. *Bow Porcelain: The Collection Formed by Geoffrey Freeman*. London: Lund Humphries, 1982.

Gluckman 1992
Gluckman, Dale Carolyn. *When Art Became Fashion: Kosode in Edo Japan*. Los Angeles: Los Angeles County Museum of Art, 1992.

Godden 1979
Godden, Geoffrey. *Oriental Export Market Porcelain and Its Influence on European Wares*. London: Granada, 1979.

Guth 1996
Guth, Christine. *Art of Edo Japan: The Artist and the City, 1615–1868*. New York: Harry N. Abrams, 1996.

Hanley 1997
Hanley, Susan B. *Everyday Things in Premodern Japan: The Hidden Legacy of Material Culture*. Berkeley: University of California Press, 1997.

Harrison 1979
Harrison, Barbara. *Swatow*. Leeuwarden, Netherlands: Gemeentelijk Museum het Princessehof, 1979.

Harrison-Hall 2001
Harrison-Hall, Jessica. *Catalogue of Late Yuan and Ming Ceramics in the British Museum*. London: British Museum, 2001.

Hayashiya and Trubner 1977
Hayashiya, Seizo, and Harry Trubner. *Chinese Ceramics from Japanese Collections, T'ang through Ming Dynasties*. New York: Asia Society, 1977.

Hinton and Impey 1989
Hinton, Mark, and Oliver Impey. *Kakiemon Porcelain from the English Country House*. London: Christie, Manson & Woods, 1989.

Idemitsu Museum 1984
Idemitsu Museum. *The Inter-Influence of Ceramic Art in East and West*. Tokyo: Idemitsu Museum, 1984.

Idemitsu Museum 2004
——. *Ko-Kutani*. Tokyo: Idemitsu Museum, 2004.

Impey 1973
Impey, Oliver. "A Tentative Classification of the Arita Kilns." In *International Symposium on Japanese Ceramics*, edited by Harry Trubner, pp. 85–91. Seattle, 1973.

Impey 1984
——. "Shoki-Imari and Tianqi: Arita and Jingdezhen in Competition for the Japanese Market in Porcelain in the Second Quarter of the Seventeenth Century." *Mededelingenblad Nederlandse Vereniging van Vrieden van de Ceramiek* 116 (1984): pp. 15–29.

Impey 1990a
——. "Japanese Export Figures in Light of Recent Excavations in Arita." *Oriental Art* 136 (1990): pp. 66–76.

Impey 1990b
——. "The Trade in Japanese Porcelain." In Ayers, Impey and Mallet 1990, pp. 15–24.

Impey 1990c
——. "Japanese Export Porcelain." In Ayers, Impey and Mallet 1990.

Impey 1996
——. *The Early Porcelain Kilns of Japan: Arita in the First Half of the Seventeenth Century*. Oxford: Clarendon Press, 1996.

Impey 1997
——. Foreword in Barry Davies 1997.

Impey 2002a
——. *Japanese Export Porcelain: Catalogue of the Collection of the Ashmolean Museum, Oxford*. Amsterdam: Hotei Publishing, 2002.

Impey 2002b
——. "Japanese Porcelain at Burghley House: The Inventory of 1688 and the Sale of 1888." *Metropolitan Museum Journal* 37 (2002): pp. 117–31.

Impey 2005
——. "Kakiemon." *Transactions of the Oriental Ceramic Society* 68 (2003–2004). London, 2005.

Impey and Tregear 1983
Impey, Oliver, and Mary Tregear. "Provenance studies of Tianqi porcelain." *Trade Ceramics Studies* 3 (1983): pp. 103–14.

Jacob Stodel 1993
Jacob Stodel. *The Splendour of Dutch Delftware: An Exhibition of 17th and 18th Century Delft Tin-Glazed Earthenware*. London: Jacob Stodel, 1993.

Jansen 1992
Jansen, Marius B. *China in the Tokugawa World*. Cambridge, MA: Harvard University Press, 1992.

Jansen 2000
——. *The Making of Modern Japan*. Cambridge: Harvard University Press, 2000.

Japan Society 1986
Japan Society. *The Burghley Porcelains: An Exhibition from the Burghley House Collection and Based on the 1688 Inventory and 1690 Devonshire Schedule*. New York: Japan Society, 1986.

Jenkins 1993
Jenkins, Donald. *The Floating World Revisited*. Portland: Portland Art Museum, 1993.

Jenyns 1965
Jenyns, Soame. *Japanese Porcelain*. London: Faber and Faber, 1965.

Jörg 1982
Jörg, Christiaan. *Porcelain and the Dutch China Trade*. The Hague: Martinus Nijhoff, 1982.

Jörg 1984
——. *Interaction in Ceramics: Oriental Porcelain and Delftware*. Hong Kong: Hong Kong Museum of Art, 1984.

Jörg 1992
——. "Japanese Apothecary Bottles with Initials." *The Hyakunenan Journal of Porcelain Study (Hyakunenan Toji Ronshu)* 7 (1992).

Jörg 1993
——. "Chinese Porcelain for the Dutch in the Seventeenth Century: Trading Networks and Private Enterprise." In *The Porcelains of Jingdezhen: Colloquies on Art & Archaeology in Asia No. 16*, edited by R.E. Scott, pp. 183–94. London: Percival David Foundation, 1993.

Jörg 2001
——."To the Highest Bidder: The Auction of a Porcelain Shop in Amsterdam in 1778." *Transactions of the Oriental Ceramic Society* 65 (2001): pp. 61–72.

Jörg 2003
——. *Fine and Curious: Japanese Export Porcelains in Dutch Collections.* Amsterdam: Hotei Publishing, 2003.

Jörg and Flecker 2001
Jörg, Christiaan, and Michael Flecker. *Porcelain from the Vung Tau Wreck: The Hallstrom Excavation.* Singapore: Sun Tree, 2001.

Kawazu 1807
Kawazu, Yoshimichi. *Suiyo shoroku.* 1807.

Keyes 1984
Keyes, Roger. *Japanese Woodblock Prints: The Ainsworth Collection.* Oberlin, Ohio: Allen Memorial Art Museum, 1984.

Kilburn 1981
Kilburn, Richard. *Transitional Wares and Their Forerunners.* Hong Kong: Hong Kong Museum of Art, 1981.

Kilburn 1988
——. "The Hatcher Junk (1643–46)." In *The Hatcher Porcelain Cargoes: The Complete Record,* by Colin Sheaf and Richard Kilburn, pp. 12–79. Oxford: Phaidon, 1988.

Kyoto National Museum 2006
Kyoto National Museum. *Kyoto Ware: Ceramic Designs and Techniques for the Capital.* Kyoto: Kyoto National Museum, 2006.

Kyushu Ceramic Museum 1984
Kyushu Ceramic Museum, ed. *Kamanotsuji, Dambagiri, Chokichidani: Investigation Report of Kiln Sites in the Hizen Region.* Arita: Kyushu Ceramic Museum, 1984.

Kyushu Ceramic Museum 1990
——. *Shibata Collection v. 1.* Arita: Kyushu Ceramic Museum, 1990.

Kyushu Ceramic Museum 1991
——. *Shibata Collection v. 2.* Arita: Kyushu Ceramic Museum, 1991.

Kyushu Ceramic Museum 1993
——. *Shibata Collection v. 3.* Arita: Kyushu Ceramic Museum, 1993.

Kyushu Ceramic Museum 1995
——. *Shibata Collection v. 4.* Arita: Kyushu Ceramic Museum, 1995.

Kyushu Ceramic Museum 1996
——. *The Kyushu Ceramic Museum Collection.* Arita: Kyushu Ceramic Museum, 1996.

Kyushu Ceramic Museum 1997
——. *Shibata Collection v. 5.* Arita: Kyushu Ceramic Museum, 1997.

Kyushu Ceramic Museum 1998
——. *Shibata Collection v. 6.* Arita: Kyushu Ceramic Museum, 1998.

Kyushu Ceramic Museum 1999
——. *Kakiemon: The Whole Aspect of the Kakiemon Style.* Arita: Kyushu Ceramic Museum, 1999.

Kyushu Ceramic Museum 2000
——. *The Voyage of Old Imari Porcelains.* Arita: Kyushu Ceramic Museum, 2000.

Kyushu Ceramic Museum 2006
——. *Shogun-ke e no kenjo Nabeshima: Nihon jiki no saikoho.* Arita: Kyushu Ceramic Museum, 2006.

Lahaussois 1997
Lahaussois, Christine. *Porcelaines de Saint-Cloud.* Paris: Union centrale des arts décoratifs, 1997.

Lahaussois 1998
——. *Faiences de Delft.* Paris: Editions de la réunion des musées nationaux, 1998.

Lang 1983
Lang, Gordon. *Wrestling Boys: An Exhibition of Chinese and Japanese Ceramics from the 16th to the 18th Century in the Collection at Burghley House.* Stamford: Burghley House Preservation Trust, 1983.

Lange 2001
Lange, Amanda E. *Delftware at Historic Deerfield, 1600–1800.* Deerfield: Historic Deerfield, 2001.

Lawrence 1997
Lawrence, Louis. *Hirado: Prince of Porcelains.* Chicago: Art Media Resources, 1997.

Le Corbeiller 1992
Le Corbeiller, Clare. Review of Ayers, Impey and Mallet 1990. *Journal of the History of Collections* 4, no. 1 (1992): pp. 150–52.

LeDuc 1996
LeDuc, Geneviève. *Porcelaine tendre de Chantilly au XVIIIe siècle.* Paris: Hazan, 1996.

Lippert 1987
Lippert, Catherine Beth. *Eighteenth-Century English Porcelain in the Collection of the Indianapolis Museum of Art.* Indianapolis: Indianapolis Museum of Art, 1987.

Little 1983
Little, Stephen. *Chinese Ceramics of the Transitional Period, 1620–1683.* New York: China Institute Gallery, 1983.

Lunsingh Scheurleer 1974
Lunsingh Scheurleer, D.F. *Chinese Export Porcelain.* New York: Pitman Publishing, 1974.

Lunsingh Scheurleer 1984
——. *Delft: Niederländische Fayence.* Munich: Klinkhardt & Biermann, 1984.

Mallet 1990
Mallet, John. "European Ceramics and the Influence of Japan." In Ayers, Impey and Mallet 1990, pp. 35–55.

Mason 1993
Mason, Penelope. *History of Japanese Art.* New York: Harry N. Abrams, 1993.

McKee 2006
McKee, Daniel. *Japanese Poetry Prints: Surimono from the Schoff Collection.* Ithaca, New York: Herbert F. Johnson Museum of Art, 2006.

Meech 1999
Meech, Julia. "The Allure of Kakiemon." *Christie's New York* 15 (September 1999): pp. 8–11.

Morita 2007
Morita, Kiyoko. *The Book of Incense.* Tokyo: Kodansha International, 2007.

Murase 2003
Murase, Miyeko. *Turning Point: Oribe and the Arts of Sixteenth-Century Japan.* New York: The Metropolitan Museum of Art, 2003.

Musée Cernuschi 2007
Musée Cernuschi. *Pagodes et Dragons: Exotisme et fantaisie dans l'Europe rococo, 1720–1770.* Paris: Musée Cernuschi, 2007.

Nagatake 1974
Nagatake, Takeshi. *Hizen toji no keifu.* Tokyo: Meichi Shuppan, 1974.

Nagatake 2003
——. *Classic Japanese Porcelain: Imari and Kakiemon.* Tokyo: Kodansha International, 2003.

National Museum of Japanese History 1998
National Museum of Japanese History. *Cultural History of Ceramic Ware.* Tokyo: National Museum of Japanese History, 1998.

Nelson and Impey 1994
Nelson, Christina, and Oliver Impey. "Oriental Art and French Patronage: The Foundation of the Bourbon-Condé Ceramics Collection." In *The International Ceramics Fair and Seminar.* London, 1994, pp. 36–43.

Nishida 1974
Nishida, Hiroko. *Japanese Export Porcelain during the Seventeenth and Eighteenth Century.* D.Phil. diss., Oxford University, 1974.

Ohashi 1991
Ohashi, Koji. "Changes in Hizen Porcelains in Design." In Kyushu Ceramic Museum 1991, pp. 87–97.

Okochi 1916
Okochi, Masatoshi. *Kakiemon to Iro-Nabeshima.* Tokyo, 1916.

Orlando Museum of Art 1988
Orlando Museum of Art. *Eighteenth Century Meissen Porcelain from the Collection of Gertrude J. and Robert T. Anderson.* Orlando: Orlando Museum of Art, 1988.

Pietsch 1993
Pietsch, Ulrich. *Early Meissen Porcelain: A Private Collection.* Lübeck: Museum für Kunst und Kulturgeschichte, 1993.

Reichel 1981
Reichel, Friedrich. *Early Japanese Porcelain: Arita Porcelain in the Dresden Collection.* London: Orbis Publishing, 1981.